SINCLA… …ROTHY

with

Gratitude and Affection

The Bible

The Bible

God's Inerrant Word

Banner Mini-Guides

Key Truths

Derek W. H. Thomas

THE BANNER OF TRUTH TRUST

THE BANNER OF TRUTH TRUST

Head Office
3 Murrayfield Road
Edinburgh
EH12 6EL
UK

North America Office
PO Box 621
Carlisle
PA 17013
USA

banneroftruth.org

First published 2018
Revised edition 2020

ISBN
Print: 978 1 84871 812 8
EPUB: 978 1 84871 813 5
Kindle: 978 1 84871 814 2

*

Typeset in 10/14 pt Minion Pro
at the Banner of Truth Trust, Edinburgh

Printed in the USA by
Versa Press, Inc.,
East Peoria, IL

Contents

Acknowledgements

Heartfelt thanks are due to the following people for the part they played in helping me write this book. First, my thanks are extended to my dear friend, Mark Johnston, who invited me to contribute to the Banner Mini-Guides series. His loyal friendship over four decades has meant more to me than I can say. Bill and Nancy Neely, and Grady and Linda Smith both loaned me their 'getaway' homes—one, in the mountains of North Carolina, the other, on the Atlantic seaboard—both ideal locations to focus and hide from the ever-intrusive cell phone. And Debbie Thompson proof-read the manuscript with an eye to detail that I do not possess, and an ability to point out 'danglers' and 'unspecified modifiers' with the gentlest of touches for a bruised ego. To all these, I am grateful beyond words and trust our team effort will contribute in some small way to the advancement of the kingdom of God.

I have known Sinclair B. Ferguson for over forty years. He encouraged me to write my first book in the early 1980s. Since then, our lives have intertwined in remarkable ways, not least when I served as 'the evening preacher' at a time when he was the Senior Minister at First Presbyterian

Church, Columbia, South Carolina. Those two years have been a highlight of my life and confirmed a friendship I count as a singular and treasured blessing. Succeeding him as the Senior Minister, I daily perceive the foundations of the Christ-centred ministry he so carefully laid. He has been and continues to be a mentor, teacher, encourager and, more importantly, a friend. I dedicate this book to him and his equally extraordinary wife, Dorothy.

DEREK W. H. THOMAS
Reformation Day
31 October 2017

Introduction

How can we possibly believe the Bible to be the infallible and inerrant word of God in the twenty-first century? Popular belief argues that science, especially the findings of geology and the dogma of a modern, militantly atheistic form of Darwinism, has thoroughly debunked any notion of a supernatural book given to us by God. Those who still believe it to be God's word with an authority that extends over all of life are viewed as 'fundamentalists' – a term of contempt suggestive of intolerance, bigotry, and a potential threat to the peace and stability of society.

J. I Packer[1] tells the story of a man in a crowd who was seen walking round and round a hat on the ground while yelling, 'It's alive! It's alive!' When at last he picked up the hat, there underneath was a Bible. The man then launched into a sermon on the nature of Scripture as God's written word.[2] The Bible has a pulse, and through its every word God speaks with authority. What the Bible says, God says.

[1] Born in 1926, J. I. Packer is an influential evangelical theologian and author. His best-known book, *Knowing God* (1973), has been reprinted many times.

[2] J. I. Packer, *Truth and Power: The Place of Scripture in the Christian Life* (Wheaton, IL: Harold Shaw Publishers, 1996), p. 9.

The notion that the Bible is true in everything it affirms and denies is preposterous, of course, to many of our contemporaries who deny the very notion of truth itself. In our time, objective truth has often been replaced by personal opinion and feelings – so what one person feels to be true for them may not necessarily feel true for you or for anyone else.

All is not lost, though – well, not yet! Most people still believe that 2 + 2 = 4, or else they would not board aeroplanes and trust the science of aerodynamics to be a constant through time and space! But truth-claims, especially religious truth-claims, get short shrift. Generally speaking, there is little patience with a view of the Bible that, on the one hand denies a pluralistic approach to religion (all ways to 'god' are viable) and, on the other seems hopelessly adrift in a world of make-believe and fantasy (miracles, and the like).

Belief in the Bible – in its authority and total truthfulness – has been under fire from the time of Moses, but especially since the Age of Reason of the eighteenth century. The twentieth century also witnessed some of the most powerful assaults upon the Bible's claims, from both inside and outside the church. And the twenty-first century appears to be ratcheting up the assault. Hence this small book, which outlines the basic elements of the doctrine of Scripture, stands ready to defend the Bible's authenticity and authority and explain to believers the logic of its claim as truth.

My first real encounter with Scripture was opening my grandmother's brand new leather edition of the King

James Version Bible – complete with zipper. I read it with impatience and amazement. I had become a Christian only days before and was eager to find out what it said. There was much that puzzled me, and the King James translation occasionally added to my difficulties in comprehension. But I experienced what I later came to understand as the *illumination* and internal testimony (or witness) of the Holy Spirit: what I read was like no other book ever written because *it wasn't like any other book ever written!* It was, and is, the word of God.

Obviously, a book of this size cannot possibly cover every aspect and nuance of the subject. It is a 'mini-guide', one of a series that will introduce the reader to some of the major themes and issues related to the Christian faith. Each one will provide an outline of the Bible's teaching on a particular subject. They will open up a key verse or portion of Scripture for study, while not neglecting other passages related to the theme under consideration. Their goal is to whet your appetite and to encourage you to explore the subject in more detail: hence the suggestions for further reading which appear after the final chapter. However, the mini-guides will provide enough information to enlarge your understanding of a number of important subjects.

All the mini-guides have been arranged in a thirteen-chapter format so that they will seamlessly fit into the teaching quarters of the church year and be useful for Sunday School lessons or Bible class studies.

While writing this mini-guide there were times when I was extremely conscious of passing over the topics at great speed for fear that if I slowed the pace the book would rapidly exceed the publisher's guidelines. I trust, however, that its brevity will help readers grasp the bigger truths of what the Bible is and what the Bible is for. May this little book help you read the Bible and fall in love with it, so that you will want to say with the psalmist – 'Oh how I love your law! It is my meditation all the day' (Psa. 119:97).

1

The Bible Is God Speaking

But he answered, 'It is written, "Man shall not live by bread alone, but by every word that comes from the mouth of God."' – Matthew 4:4

Christians believe that God communicates through the Bible. Christians believe much more than that about the Bible; but they believe no less. Through its pages, its sentences, and its words, God speaks. In the Scriptures of the Old and New Testaments, God reveals himself and his purposes for human beings and creation in general.

In the pages of the *Holy Bible*, God's plans concerning creation, the fall, redemption, and judgment are disclosed in varying and progressive detail.

The Bible's unique witness to what God has done in history (what Bible scholars often refer to as 'redemptive history'), together with the unshakable testimony given to the Bible by the church for two thousand years, invests Scripture with a certain 'authority' above other sources of information.

God speaks in creation

Before we examine God's *special* revelation in Scripture, we need to begin a little further back. Christians also believe that God speaks in creation itself. The rocks and hills, the rivers and seas, testify to God's being. The apostle Paul tells of just how comprehensive this testimony is in the world about us:

> For what can be known about God is plain to them, because God has shown it to them. For his invisible attributes, namely, his eternal power and divine nature, have been clearly perceived, ever since the creation of the world, in the things that have been made (Rom. 1:19, 20).

Many centuries before Paul, David, the great king of Israel and the author of many of the Old Testament Psalms, testified in similar fashion:

> The heavens declare the glory of God,
> and the sky above proclaims his handiwork.
> Day to day pours out speech,
> and night to night reveals knowledge.
> There is no speech, nor are there words,
> whose voice is not heard.
> Their measuring line goes out through all the earth,
> and their words to the end of the world (Psa. 19:1-4).

In an instant, at the sight of a sunset, or the beauty of a bird or an animal in motion, or the sound of music, the goodness and majesty of God come to light in a way that evokes awe and wonder. Unbelievers may describe this phenomenon in different ways, but when we are given a new heart by the Holy Spirit, when faith sees and hears and feels these sublime moments, we describe them differently.

> Heaven above is softer blue
>   Earth around is sweeter green;
> Something lives in every hue
>   Christless eyes have never seen;
> Birds with gladder songs o'erflow,
>   Flow'rs with deeper beauties shine,
> Since I know, as now I know,
>   I am His, and He is mine.[1]

God's revelation in creation (sometimes referred to as *general revelation*) is more than merely an external testimony to God's existence and power. The revelation of God also penetrates *within* us, to the very core of our being and consciousness.

Such is the comprehensive nature of the revelation (or disclosure) that God makes in creation, the apostle Paul concludes that no human being is 'without excuse' (Rom. 1:20). No one, no matter how culturally primitive or ignorant of the teachings of the Bible, is devoid of God's self-disclosure in the natural world, for God's 'eternal power and divine nature' are apparent everywhere. Every human being knows God, for what 'can be known' (what is *knowable*, Rom. 1:19) is 'plain' and can be clearly seen. Unbelievers know that God exists and that he will hold

[1] From the hymn, *Loved With Everlasting Love*, by George Wade Robinson (1838–77).

them to account, no matter how much they may protest otherwise.

People do protest, of course. The unbeliever 'exchanges' the truth of God for a lie, and turns creation itself into an idol to be worshipped (Rom. 1:23, 25). Despite any self-aggrandizing claims of wisdom, this is sheer folly on man's part, wilful and culpable folly (Rom. 1:22). And the folly may rise to the level of denying God's very existence. But God does not believe in atheists![1]

The revelation of God in creation also manifests itself *within us*. In addition to the revelation of God *out there*, there is also the revelation of who we are and what we are as human beings made in the image of God (Gen. 1:26, 27). Our first parents not only experienced a Paradise that expressed the glory of God, they were also conscious of something very special within – the knowledge that God had made them and that they were created to reflect his glory in worship and praise. The revelation of God ensured that not only were they *spectators* of this drama, they were also *actors* in it.[2]

God speaks into creation

Over and above the revelation of God in creation (*general revelation*) is the revelation of God *into* creation (*special*

[1] I have borrowed these words from the title of John Blanchard's book, *Does God Believe in Atheists?* (EP Books, 2011, 2nd edition).

[2] One is reminded of Abraham Kuyper's statement, 'If the cosmos is the theatre of revelation, in this theatre man is both actor and spectator.' *Encyclopedia of Sacred Theology*, tr. J. H. de Vries (New York: Funk & Wagnalls, 1900), p. 264.

revelation). It is 'special' because this revelation refers to that which cannot be gained by sight, or sound, or perception, or reason. Even in man's sinless condition before the Fall, there were things about God that could not be known by the human eye or ear or mind. This is information that must penetrate creation from outside of it.

Such special content was delivered by *special agents*: patriarchs (e.g. Abraham, Isaac, Jacob), prophets (e.g. Moses, Elijah, Isaiah), and apostles (e.g. Peter, John, Paul) spoke as though God himself spoke through them. The expressions 'God said' or 'Thus says the Lord' occur several thousand times in Scripture.[1] The author of the letter to the Hebrews testifies to a long line of special agents who spoke God's word: 'Long ago, at many times and in many ways, God spoke to our fathers by the prophets' (Heb. 1:1). Men such as Moses, David, Isaiah, and Ezekiel testified to being conduits through whom God himself spoke.

Those who receive God's special revelation are also themselves *special* or unique. For not everyone receives it. This revelation cannot be known unless its content is proclaimed (in written or verbal form). Paul addresses the issue explicitly:

> But how are they to call on him in whom they have not believed? And how are they to believe in him of whom they have never heard? And how are they to hear without someone preaching? And how are they to preach unless

[1] See, for example, Exod. 14:1; 20:1; Lev. 4:1; Num. 4:1; Deut. 4:2; 32:48; Isa. 1:10, 24; Jer. 1:11; Ezek. 1:3.

they are sent? As it is written, 'How beautiful are the feet of those who preach the good news!' (Rom. 10:14, 15).

Special delivery

In addition to special agents and special content, *special delivery systems* are employed in giving special revelation. God spoke through his mighty actions and demonstrations of his power. In the exodus of the people of Israel from Egypt and in their exile to captivity in Babylon, as also in the birth of Jesus at Bethlehem and the death of Jesus at Calvary, and the descent of the Holy Spirit on the Day of Pentecost, God unveiled his plan and purpose in ways that could not have been discerned otherwise.

On some special occasions God appeared temporarily in human form. The expression 'the angel of the Lord' occurs over two hundred times in the Old Testament, although about half of these occurrences refer to heavenly messengers rather than to appearances of God himself. But in some instances, the identity of the angel is clearly said to be the Lord himself. Such occasions, when the 'angel of the Lord' clearly refers to God himself, are referred to as *theophanies*.

In Genesis 16, for example, 'the angel of the Lord' finds the Egyptian maidservant of Abraham's wife Sarah in the wilderness, and speaks to her. Later in the same chapter we read that Hagar 'called the name of the LORD who spoke to her, "You are a God of seeing," for she said, "Truly here I have seen him who looks after me."'[1] Clearly,

[1] See also Gen. 22:15 (Abraham); Exod. 3:2 (Moses); Num. 22:22 (Balaam).

Hagar understood the encounter as a divine visitation, the manifestation of God to a human being.

Sometimes the revelation came in the form of visions, either external or internal. We are told in 1 Samuel 9:9, for example, that a 'prophet' used to be called 'a seer', for the uncomplicated reason that the prophets 'saw' things. Prophets of a later era in Israel's history also saw visions. For example, Isaiah was given a vision in which he saw the overwhelming and intimidating holiness of the sovereign God (Isa. 6).[1] Ezekiel saw a vision of a fantastical chariot-throne of the Lord of glory (Ezek. 1). The apostle Peter was given a vision of a sheet in which there were both 'clean' and 'unclean animals' (Acts 10:9-16). By this vision God was revealing to Peter the abolition of Old Testament ceremonial law which had been a barrier that had separated Jews from Gentiles. The apostle John frequently employs a verb in the book of Revelation which suggests that he *saw* things: 'And I saw ...' (Rev. 1:12, 17; 5:1, 2, 6; 6:9, etc.).

Sometimes, God revealed his will in dreams. Joseph, for example, rises to great prominence in Egypt as an interpreter of Pharaoh's dreams (Gen. 40). Similarly, Daniel (also known as Belteshazzar) interpreted the dreams of King Nebuchadnezzar of Babylon (Dan. 4).

The principal way special revelation was given, however, was through prophecy. God raised up prophets from among the people of Israel and through them he brought

[1] John tells us that this was a vision of Christ (John 12:41).

his word to the people. A prophet was a 'spokesperson'.[1] The biblical scholar Geerhardus Vos (1862–1949) defined a prophet thus: 'a prophet is an authorized spokesperson for the Deity in whose word a divinely communicated power resides.'[2] Prophets engaged in both forth-telling (as in preaching and expounding God's law) and foretelling (indicating future events). Customarily, the prophets did the former more than the latter in expounding God's will (as in preaching). Moses was a prophet, but his role was almost exclusively that of a forth-teller, one who taught God's law, rather than a foreteller, one who predicted future events (Deut. 18:15, 18).

Prophets spoke what God told them to speak. The revelation of God's will through them, alongside that which was later communicated through Christ's apostles, provided a solid foundation for the life, witness, and growth of the church. Christians are 'built on the *foundation* of the apostles and prophets, Christ Jesus himself being the cornerstone' (Eph. 2:20).

Revelation in Christ

The incarnation of the Son of God – when the Son took 'human form' and was 'born in the likeness of men' (Phil. 2:6-8) – was a unique moment of the revelation of God in history. The author of the letter to the Hebrews says that the coming of God's Son into the world marks the beginning of a period of time known as the 'last days' (Heb. 1:1, 2).

[1] In Hebrew, *navi*.

[2] Geerhardus Vos, *Biblical Theology* (1948; repr. Edinburgh: Banner of Truth Trust, 1975), p. 193.

Christ's coming signalled the fulfilment of a promise God made in the garden of Eden, that in the 'seed of the woman' (Jesus Christ) a decisive and fatal blow would be given to the serpent's (Satan's) head (Gen. 3:15). The incarnation of the Son of God is a revelation of the loving heart of God the Father towards his rebellious creatures (John 3:16; Rom. 8:32). The person of Jesus himself, as well as his words and actions, is a revelation of the Father's nature:

> Whoever has seen me has seen the Father (John 14:9).

> For God, who said, 'Let light shine out of darkness', has shone in our hearts to give the light of the knowledge of the glory of God in the face of Jesus Christ (2 Cor. 4:6).

Since Jesus is God revealed in flesh, everything about his character shows us what God is like. As John so eloquently put it in the prologue to his Gospel account of Jesus, 'No one has ever seen God; the only God, who is at the Father's side, *he has made him known*' (John 1:18).

Revelation in Scripture

In theory, God's special revelation could have been preserved apart from the use of Scripture. God could have ensured that his truth be kept through oral tradition alone. Certainly, for lengthy periods of history (the decades before the New Testament was written, for example), this is precisely what took place. In the first chapter of the *Westminster Confession of Faith* this very truth is helpfully stated:

> It pleased the Lord, at sundry times, and in divers manners, to reveal himself, and to declare his will unto his church;

> and afterwards for the better preserving and propagating of the truth, and for the more sure establishment and comfort of the church against the corruption of the flesh, and the malice of Satan and of the world, *to commit the same wholly unto writing*; which makes the Holy Scripture to be most necessary; those former ways of God's revealing his will unto his people being now ceased.[1]

God, in his wisdom and grace, ensured that special revelation was written down, for the 'perfecting' of the church. He determined that we should have a written record of all that must be known and believed for our full salvation. In our own time it is surely a great privilege to have access to the mind of God in written form – whether printed or electronic.

So although abundant evidence exists all around us of the existence and character of God, not everything is revealed in creation. There are some things we need to know that are only revealed in the Bible. The gospel is one of them.

[1] *Westminster Confession of Faith*, I.1 (emphasis added).

2

The Bible and Words

And God spoke all these words, saying ...

– Exodus 20:1

On Mount Sinai God gave Moses words which he had not only spoken but also written. We read that God said to Moses, 'Come up to me on the mountain and wait there, that I may give you the tablets of stone ... *which I have written*' (Exod. 24:12).

There is no getting away from it: the Bible is a book of words ... over half a million in the original languages of the Old and New Testament texts, rising to over three-quarters of a million in the English Standard Version translation.

Nouns, verbs, adjectives, conjunctions. Words with structure – sentences, logical arguments, statements, poetry. Words have meaning, *precise* meaning. And there's the rub, for in our post-modern era, such a statement about words possessing precise meaning is often doubted and frequently denied (even though the statement 'words have no precise meaning' is understood by post-modern doubters to convey something precise and meaningful!).

According to the influential German philosopher Immanuel Kant (1724–1804), what exists in the world beyond our senses (the *noumena*) cannot break into the world we experience from day to day (the *phenomena*).[1] If God exists, he cannot speak directly into this world. Twentieth-century thinkers took his ideas further, suggesting that if meaning cannot be ascertained from outside this world, then neither can it be attained within it. Language itself is too inadequate a vehicle to convey true meaning. The sociologists argued that language is itself a human phenomenon, an evolutionary experience that grew out of primitive grunts and groans into more sophisticated words with localized and fluid meaning.

Poets such as Gertrude Stein (1874–1946) wrote 'a rose is a rose is a rose is a rose' and 'there is no there there', insisting that no objective grand narrative (or meta-narrative) exists.[2] Novelists such as Franz Kafka (1883–1924) suggested that human beings find themselves in a vortex of despair and disappointment from which escape is not possible. The term 'Kafkaesque' suggests the illogical nature of our existence.[3] And there's the Irish poet-playwright, Samuel Beckett (1906–89), whose play *Waiting for Godot* suggests a world that is essentially absurd and devoid of meaning.

[1] See Immanuel Kant, *Critique of Pure Reason*, Penguin Classics (London: Penguin Random House, 2008).

[2] Part of the 1913 poem 'Sacred Emily', which appeared in the 1922 book *Geography and Plays*.

[3] For a summary of Kafka's thought, see Carolin Duttlinger, *The Cambridge Introduction to Franz Kafka* (Cambridge: Cambridge University Press, 2013), pp. 2-13.

Philosophers such as Ludwig Wittgenstein (1889–1951) and A. J. Ayer (1910–89) expressed similar doubts about meaning.[1] Perhaps the most famous expression of this doubt is the set of four poems by T. S. Eliot (published between 1941 and 1943) in which he wrote these lines:

> Words strain,
> Crash and sometimes break, under the burden,
> Under the tension, slip, slide, perish,
> Decay with imprecision, will not stay in place,
> Will not stay still.[2]

The point of Eliot's poem is that words have no objective meaning. And yet thousands have read his words, gleaned their meaning, and either agreed or disagreed with what he wrote. These words mean *something* – something the reader either agrees with or dislikes intensely. In a more popular refrain, the character Humpty Dumpty (in the nonsense, fantasy world of Lewis Carroll's *Alice's Adventures in Wonderland*) argued that words mean what we tell them to mean, no more and no less.[3]

[1] See L. Wittgenstein, *Tractatus Logico-Philosophicus*, tr. O. F. Pears and B. F. McGuinness (London: Routledge & Kegan Paul, 1961); A. J. Ayer, *Language, Truth, and Logic* (1936; repr. London: Penguin Publications, 1990).

[2] The lines come in the first of the four poems, *Burnt Norton*.

[3] L. Carroll, *Through the Looking-Glass* (Raleigh, NC: Hayes Barton Press, 1872), p. 72. *Through the Looking-Glass, and What Alice Found There*, published in 1871, was the sequel to *Alice's Adventures in Wonderland*, published in 1865. They were written by the English mathematician Charles Lutwidge Dodgson under the pseudonym Lewis Carroll. They tell of a girl named Alice who fell through a rabbit hole into a fantasy world populated by very strange, anthropomorphic creatures.

The idea that words have no objective meaning has led to many different conclusions. In an attempt to avoid total despair the German theologian Friedrich Schleiermacher (1768–1834) developed the idea of the objectivity of experience. Religion, he wrote, consists in 'a feeling of absolute dependence'. When words fail, there is always feeling.

God's words

Are we then to give up on words and trust in our feelings instead? Is it true that the only meaningful communication that exists is an experience, an emotion? Are words inadequate to convey true, objective meaning? This somewhat condensed introduction has been necessary because scepticism exists as to whether the Bible – a book of *words* – possesses any objective value. Is the Bible to be relegated to the history section of the library? Does it simply contain a record of what some people thought was true? Is it able to insist on the objectivity of truth itself?

Before we examine the nature of *all* the words in the Bible, we should ponder the more basic starting-point: the Bible contains words spoken objectively by God. These words are true, and have objective meaning, because God is true and he has meaning.

Later in this book we will consider the claims made about the *totality* of Scripture, but for now it will suffice to think about the claims made about *some* of the words in the Bible. And the claim is that they are words spoken directly through the mouth of God. Some 3,800 times the Bible employs the expression 'God said', or 'Thus says the

Lord'. Of course, not all Scripture comes to us by dictation, but some of it clearly does. These words are therefore God's words, and only a denial of the knowability of God or of his ability to break into our world can overthrow the objectivity of these words of Scripture.

Jesus and God's words

But another issue addresses the point we are making: What about Jesus' words? If Jesus is God – and the Bible claims that he is – his words, of necessity, must carry divine authority. Some may quibble over how accurately his words are recorded in Scripture, but if any consensus exists as to their authenticity, then these, too, are God's words. The tradition of printing Jesus' words in red is not a good one (because they invest these words with greater importance than the rest of Scripture), but the point being made here is that the existence of the 'words of Jesus' means that the Bible contains words spoken by God himself.

Furthermore, in Revelation chapters 2 and 3, Jesus dictates letters to the apostle John, who writes them down word for word and delivers them to the churches in Asia Minor.[1] Jesus Christ, the incarnate Son of God (risen and ascended in Revelation, but incarnate still), speaks as God himself in human flesh. His words – nouns, verbs, adjectives, adverbs – are words with true, objective meaning. They do not slip and slide, or change with the shifting course of history. When Jesus speaks, God speaks. To doubt the authenticity of these words as God's words is

[1] Note the imperative 'write' in Rev. 2:1, 8, 12, 18; 3:1, 7, 14.

to doubt more than merely the nature of Scripture; it calls into question the identity and knowability of Christ, the Christ who (according to Scripture) is none other than the Lord, the covenant God himself.[1]

Furthermore, it is not simply an issue of words spoken by Jesus; we also need to consider his own estimation of Bible words – in his case, the words of the Old Testament. Some ninety times the expression 'it is written' or its equivalent occurs in the New Testament. Pertinent to the point we are making here is the use Jesus made of this expression, asserting thereby his complete and utter confidence in the source and objective meaning of these words.

In the narratives which record Christ's temptation in the wilderness, we see the devil in his most beguiling and threatening form coming against Jesus. On three occasions Jesus met Satan's temptation with quotations from the Bible. He prefaces each quotation with the words, 'It is written' (see Matt. 4:4, 7, 10).[2] According to Jesus the words of Scripture come from the mouth of God. The Scriptures quoted bring all discussion and equivocation to an end; God's words put an end to all debate and uncertainty.

Take a moral issue such as divorce. When the Pharisees asked Jesus for a ruling on the matter of divorce and remarriage, his response was instant: 'Have you not read . . .?' (Matt.

[1] Simply to provide one example: Paul's statement in Philippians 2:11 makes the claim that Jesus Christ is 'Lord', using the Greek term *kurios*, which was the term employed in the Greek translation of the Old Testament to render the divine name (*Yahweh*).

[2] It should also be noted that Satan himself employed the same expression in citing Scripture (Matt. 4:6).

19:4), and proceeded to draw their attention to what Moses had written in Genesis 1:27 and 2:24. The lesson is clear: moral disputes are solved by reference to words written in Scripture, words that carry divine authority.

Jesus viewed his death as a matter of Scripture fulfilment: 'The Son of Man goes *as it is written* of him', he taught (Matt. 26:24). His betrayal took place to fulfil the Scripture (John 13:18). The fact that he was hated by the Jews without a cause was to fulfil what was written in the Scriptures (John 15:25). When encouraged to escape the painful rigours of crucifixion and death, he carefully pointed out to his disciples that Scripture had predicted the precise manner of his death and therefore he must comply: 'But how then should the Scriptures be fulfilled, that it must be so?' (Matt. 26:54).

There is much to be said about the divine origin of *all* Scripture, but it is a necessary and decisive starting-point to see that *some* words of Scripture clearly specify their divine origin. As far as Jesus was concerned the Old Testament in its entirety was the word of God. John Stott (1921–2011), the British evangelical leader, summarizes the point well: 'The reason why the church has historically submitted to Scripture, and why evangelicals continue to do so, is that our Lord Jesus himself did.'[1] And again: 'If we wish to submit to the authority of Christ, we must submit to the authority of Scripture.'[2]

[1] John Stott, *Evangelical Truth: A Personal Plea for Unity* (Leicester: IVP, 1999), p. 69.

[2] *Ibid.*, p. 70.

This chapter began with an investigation into the possibility of objective meaning of the written or spoken word. It is a subject that has been disputed by intellectuals for over a century and has brought us into what some call *late-modernity* or *post-modernity*. Scepticism about objective meaning calls into question any claim the Bible (or any other book for that matter) makes about itself. The investigation of the nature of Scripture must therefore address the nature of meaning and dispel the doubt that exists. The elephant in the room is the fact that all such discussion employs arguments and opinions that involve the use of words which have very precise meaning indeed. There is, therefore, an irony, not to say a contradiction, in the existence of the very debate itself!

God has revealed himself in words – the words of Scripture. These words are true and trustworthy. Jesus thought so, and if he is not correct about this, then more things are at stake than merely the nature of Scripture. Our very salvation is called into question, for if Jesus is wrong about the divine source of Old Testament words, then might he not be wrong about other matters too? The logic is deadly and must be avoided. Better, by far, to trust Jesus on this matter, for any other posture leads only to despair.

Those who trust Jesus Christ and follow him as their divine Lord will hold fast to his teaching about the Bible being the word of God.

3

The Bible and Progressive Revelation

Long ago, at many times and in many ways, God spoke to our fathers by the prophets, but in these last days he has spoken to us by his Son, whom he appointed the heir of all things, through whom also he created the world. – Hebrews 1:1, 2

Our knowledge of God is the direct result of the things he has chosen to make known to us about himself through revelation. Whether in creation, in Christ, or in Scripture, God has revealed things to us and in us which would otherwise remain hidden and unknown. What we know about Christ (and what he reveals of the character of God), we know only because Scripture has kept a record of it for us to read and study.

But God has not revealed all his secrets to us. Some things, many things, he has kept hidden. 'The secret things belong to the LORD our God, but the things that are revealed belong to us and to our children forever, that we may do all the words of this law' (Deut. 29:29). While we know some things about God and his ways, we know only a little.

Nor has God disclosed what is knowable about him and his ways *all at once*. Like a kind and thoughtful father, our heavenly Father makes us wait, and thereby encourages us to grow, as he slowly, little by little, makes himself and his ways known to us. The truth of *progressive revelation* is apparent in the words that preface the book of Hebrews:

> Long ago, at many times and in many ways, God spoke to our fathers by the prophets, but in these last days he has spoken to us by his Son (Heb. 1:1, 2).

As we saw in our first chapter, God's revelation is given progressively, cumulatively, and, in a sense, finally in his Son. Initially, God revealed himself in ways that are best suited for children 'under age', employing such modes of communication as dreams and visions, but 'in these last days' God has spoken with greater clarity and insight, and in a manner suggesting that no further revelation of this kind is to be expected.

Shadow and type

One of the most obvious ways in which progress is seen in the unfolding of divine revelation in Scripture is the transition from the Old Testament to the New Testament. What is anticipated in the Old is manifest in the New. The ceremonial aspects of the old covenant served as a 'copy and shadow' of things to come (Heb. 8:5). Events and circumstances in the Old Testament served as 'types', written down for our instruction (1 Cor. 10:11).[1] As New Testament scholar Vern Poythress (1946–) explains,

> A 'type' in the language of theology, *is a special example, symbol, or picture that God designed beforehand, and that he placed in history at an earlier point in time in order to point forward to a later, larger fulfilment.*[2]

The bloody sacrifices of animals in the Old Testament anticipated the death and *once*-offered sacrifice of Christ in the New (Heb. 9:7, 12, 26, 27, 28; Greek, *hapax*). There is a clear progress from type to antitype in the ushering in of the new covenant.

The idea of progress

In an enigmatic and often misunderstood statement in the prologue to John's Gospel, we read the following: 'For the law was given through Moses; grace and truth came through Jesus Christ' (John 1:17). Clearly, the apostle John does not intend us to draw the conclusion that the Mosaic era contained no hint of grace or that the period of the New Testament contains no demand of law. John is drawing a *relative* contrast in absolute terms.

In much the same way, the apostle Paul makes similar observations about the Mosaic era as a 'ministry of death'

[1] The word 'type' (example, ESV) is used twice in this passage, 1 Cor. 10:6, 11.

[2] Vern. S. Poythress, 'A Survey of the History of Salvation', in *Understanding Scripture: An Overview of the Bible's Origin, Reliability, and Meaning*, eds. Wayne Grudem, C. John Collins and Thomas S. Schreiner (Wheaton, IL: Crossway, 2012), p. 177.

and 'condemnation' (2 Cor. 3:7, 9). Paul does not intend us to draw the conclusion that no grace existed in the Mosaic period or that the entire era consisted in a works-based view of justification. But there is a sense in which the purpose of this epoch was to reinforce mankind's inability to save itself by human effort and initiative. In contrast with the New Testament, the Mosaic era appears repressive and condemnatory.

These examples demonstrate how God reveals his truth with varying emphases in different epochs. Indeed, as we examine the history of the world from Eden onwards, we can discern different ages or aeons. We may, for example, without characterizing differences with any degree of precision, discern unique stages of history such as the Patriarchal, Mosaic, Davidic, Prophetic, and Incarnational, in which particular truths received a greater degree of attention.

Some truths come relatively quickly: the universality and extent of sin, for example, in the opening chapters of Genesis, reaches a definitive point in Genesis 6:5: 'The LORD saw that the wickedness of man was great in the earth, and that every intention of the thoughts of his heart was only evil continually.'

Other truths must wait. The doctrine of the resurrection of the body, for example, is not easily found in the first five books of Moses.[1] The Sadducees in Jesus' time,

[1] That is, Genesis, Exodus, Leviticus, Numbers, and Deuteronomy; also sometimes referred to as the Pentateuch (from the Greek word that simply means 'five books'), or the Torah (from the Hebrew word for 'instruction', a reminder that the five books of Moses contain more than merely 'law').

who only read the Pentateuch, did not believe in a bodily resurrection. However, it was a statement found in the book of Exodus that Jesus employed to demonstrate to the Sadducees the doctrine of resurrection.[1]

Furthermore, what may appear only as a 'seed' in earlier parts of Scripture may later be seen to have germinated and grown into a fully formed 'flower' in later parts of the Bible, the latter bearing little or no resemblance to the former.

All kinds of issues in Scripture suggest development and progress in revelation. For example, there is the difficult issue of the seeming tolerance of low levels of morality in the early periods of revelation. One such issue is the practice of polygamy. Later, Jesus explicitly argues that the divine intention 'from the very beginning' is that a man ought to be married to *one* woman (see Mark 10:2-9). The practice of taking more than one wife at the same time began with Lamech (see Gen. 4:19). There then followed a long line of polygamists which included Abraham, Jacob, Gideon, Elkanah, David, and Solomon. But polygamy was a flagrant violation of the principle set out in God's words recorded in Genesis 2:18-25. However, there seems to be a general forbearance of this sin in the pages of the Old Testament. Strictly speaking, this is more a matter of God's patience and longsuffering than a development in the ethics related to marriage and monogamy.

[1] Jesus pointed the Sadducees to Exod. 3:6: 'I am the God of your father, the God of Abraham, the God of Isaac, and the God of Jacob', adding that God was not the God of the dead, but of the living (Matt. 22:23-33).

The Trinity

The Trinity is an example of a doctrine that grew and developed in Scripture. Not only *in* Scripture, but beyond it too, as the church wrestled with the concurrence of two explicit truths: there is only *one* God, yet there is *more than one* who is this one God. A remarkable feature of the New Testament era was the ease with which Christians accepted the deity of Jesus Christ and that of the Holy Spirit. It is remarkable especially when we consider that the first authors of the New Testament, which declares that Jesus is God, were Jews. The Jews were monotheists (people who believe that there is only *one* God): three times a day they religiously repeated the words of the *Shema*: 'Hear, O Israel: The LORD our God, the LORD is one' (Deut. 6:4).

In the light of the New Testament, it is relatively easy to go back to the Old Testament and see the Trinity in a number of places: in the plural form for the general name of God (*Elohim*),[1] or the fact that in Genesis God employs the first-person plural when he says, 'Let *us* make man in *our* image, after *our* likeness' (Gen. 1:26). The truth is, however, that no Jew in the Old Testament ever concluded that God exists in some form of plurality. The plural was viewed as an expression of majesty.

We may, in fact, disagree on the extent to which *hints* of the Trinity are given in the Old Testament, but there is universal agreement that whatever hints there are were not discerned until the dawn of the New Testament era. The doctrine of the Trinity was revealed *progressively*.

[1] The *–im* suffix is a general indicator of plurality in Hebrew.

Left behind

Another indication of progress and development in the process of revelation is the way in which certain issues and themes get left behind. The idea of 'holy space', for example, was dominant in the era of the tabernacle and temple but is completely missing in the New Testament.

More fascinating is the way we perceive progress *within the New Testament itself*. There are aspects of the early church which seem utterly missing from its more mature form. The consensual sharing of material goods, for example, prominent in the post-Pentecost church of Acts 2 (verses 44-45), and dominant in the chilling narrative of the deaths of Ananias and Sapphira in Acts 5, seems altogether absent in 'mature' reflections on the characteristics of the New Testament church found in later epistles. This suggests that the issue of selling one's possessions and forming some form of cooperative agreement was either a failed experiment or, more likely, a necessary issue to ensure the growth of the initial seed of the church in a hostile and threatening environment.

Similarly, we could point to the change that takes place in evangelism in the New Testament, initially almost exclusively 'to the house of Israel' (Mark 6:7; Luke 10:1) and then decisively to the Gentiles (Acts 13:46).

More controversial is the issue of the continuation or cessation of certain gifts within *and beyond* the New Testament era. Why, for example, is no mention made of the gifts of tongues and prophecy in the distinguishing qualities of deacons or elders in the pastoral epistles?[1] Or, more pertinently perhaps, why is no mention made of the possession of these gifts as signs of Christian maturity in those passages given to such descriptions (e.g. Eph. 4:12f.; Phil. 3:12f.; Col. 1:28; 4:12; 1 Cor. 2:6; James 1:2; Rom. 8:28-29; 1 Pet. 2:2; 2 Pet. 3:18)? One answer is that the gifts of tongues and prophecy were 'signs of a true apostle' (2 Cor. 12:12) and designed to disappear along with the apostles.[2]

Continuing (progressive) revelation and the authority of Scripture

One important issue that emerges from the debate over the cessation or continuation of special revelation in the form of tongues or prophecy is the finality of Scripture in all matters relating to faith and practice. Cessationists, for example, argue that if tongues and prophecy are of the nature of 'Thus says the Lord' revelations, then their content is equal to, or even supersedes, Scripture. For this reason, some argue that the gift of prophecy in the New Testament occurs at two distinguishable levels: one that is authoritative (and on a par with Scripture) and another which only approximates to Scripture, but in no way threatens its authority.

The case of Agabus in Acts 21:10, 11 and later in 28:17 is sometimes referenced as a case of a prophecy that is less

[1] Paul's letters known as 1 and 2 Timothy and Titus were written to two men who were serving as pastors in Ephesus and Crete respectively.

[2] This is not the place to argue for or against the issue of cessationism (the term often used to argue for the disappearance of the gifts of tongues and prophecy in the New Testament era along with the apostles).

than 'Thus says the Lord'. In this prophecy, a suggestion is made that Agabus was incorrect about some of the details of Paul's arrest. This, it is said, provides an example of continuing prophecy in the church today that does not threaten the authority of Scripture. The argument is tenuous and has been soundly refuted.[1]

The point of this chapter has been to outline the *progressive* nature of revelation. This issue has important implications in understanding what the Bible – and particular sections of it rooted in a specific period of the history of redemption – has to say, particularly to us, centuries after its completion. Understanding the timeline of the Bible is vital, therefore, if we are to understand the Bible's message.

[1] For a refutation of this interpretation as given by Wayne Grudem, see Sinclair B. Ferguson, *The Holy Spirit* (Downers Grove, IL: IVP, 1996), pp. 226-229.

4

The Bible and Plenary Inspiration

All Scripture is breathed out by God and profitable for teaching, for reproof, for correction, and for training in righteousness, that the man of God may be competent, equipped for every good work. – 2 Timothy 3:16, 17

Two words in the title of this chapter require some explanation.

The first is the word *inspiration*. What do we mean when we describe the Bible as 'inspired'? Often, the meaning is thought to be that the Bible is an inspiring book, which elevates our thoughts and actions above the commonplace and routine to lofty levels otherwise unreached. This was the view advocated by the influential English poet, literary critic, philosopher and theologian Samuel Taylor Coleridge (1772–1834). That the Bible is an inspiring book in this way is of course true. The Bible should and does inspire us!

But, frankly, so do a number of other things. Speaking personally, J. R. R. Tolkien's trilogy, *The Lord of the Rings*, and Gustav Mahler's symphonic cycle are an inspiration to me. Indeed, there are a great many things (people, events, literature, music, art, sculpture, etc.) that *inspire*. But this is not what is meant when we speak of the inspiration of Scripture.

Another possibility is that God inspired *the writers* of Scripture. He moved them in some way to write. Moses, David, Isaiah, and Paul were in this sense 'inspired', and were enabled to write beyond the level of the ordinary and mundane. This, too, is true. These men were empowered by the Holy Spirit to write what they did, thereby ensuring Scripture has a quality that exceeds all other literature. But this, also, is not what is meant by the inspiration of Scripture.

The term 'inspire' was the word chosen by the translators of the King James Version of 1611 when they came to render 2 Timothy 3:16 into English: 'All scripture is given by *inspiration* of God.' Sadly, this translation fails to indicate the precise point being made by the Greek word in the original. It suggests a breathing *out* rather than a breathing *into*. The Greek word (and, for that matter, its Hebrew equivalent) may signify both 'spirit' and 'wind/breath'. All Scripture is produced by the Holy Spirit, who is described as God's creative breath. 'By the word of the LORD the heavens were made, and by the breath of his mouth all their host' (Psa. 33:6), which is 'a statement in the last words of which Christian readers rightly find a reference to the Holy Spirit, whose very name (*ruach* in Hebrew, *pneuma* in Greek) has "breath" among its meanings.'[1]

[1] J. I. Packer, *Truth and Power: The Place of Scripture in the Christian Life* (Wheaton, IL: Harold Shaw Publishers, 1996), p. 207.

The breath of God

Scripture is the product of God 'breathing out'. Putting it another way, the Bible is the breath of God. God exhales, and the product is Scripture. This is why the English Standard Version translates 2 Timothy 3:16, 17 this way: 'All Scripture is *breathed out* by God and profitable for teaching, for reproof, for correction, and for training in righteousness, that the man of God may be complete, equipped for every good work.' 'Breathed out'. Imagine the sight of your own breath on a cold morning as you take a brisk walk. That is the image in view here. Scripture is from 'the mouth of God' (Matt. 4:4). Scripture is God speaking.

In addition to the points above, 2 Timothy 3:16, 17 teaches us four truths:

First, it is teaching us something about the totality of Scripture: '*All* Scripture'. Attempts have been made to restrict the Greek for 'all Scripture' to only those parts of Scripture that demonstrate the quality of inspiration. The text would then read something like this: 'All inspired Scripture …' Such an interpretation would lead to a 'partial inspiration' view of Scripture which sees some parts inspired and other parts not. The Greek word here can be rendered as either 'all' or 'every'. If the former, then it refers to the Bible as a whole; if the latter, then it refers to the Bible in its distinct parts. Either way, no selective view of inspiration is acceptable.

This has not stopped many scholars putting forward theories of Scripture which allow for cultural accommodation of pagan mythology, or mistakes in historical and geographical details, on the assumption that the quality of inspiration varies. Their arguments suggest that some Scripture possesses the quality of inspiration ('breathed-out-ness') more than others, and some Scripture does not possess it at all. Yet the apostle Paul's statement to Timothy makes it clear that not some but *all* Scripture is from the mouth of God.

The view that all Scripture is inspired is sometimes referred to as belief in the *plenary* inspiration of Scripture (from the Latin *plenus*, meaning 'full').

What Scripture says, God says

Second, the implication of Paul's words in 2 Timothy is this: 'What Scripture says, God says.' This vitally important truth was ably set forth by the French reformer John Calvin (1509–64), who in his commentary on 2 Timothy 3:16, 17, made the following statements:

> Moses and the prophets did not utter at random what we have from their hand but, since they spoke by divine impulse, they confidently and fearlessly testified, as was actually the case, that it was the mouth of the Lord that spoke ... *We owe to Scripture the same reverence which we owe to God, because it has proceeded from him alone, and has nothing of man mixed with it.*[1]

[1] *Comm.* On 2 Tim. 3:16-17. *Calvin's New Testament Commentaries. The Second Epistle of Paul to the Corinthians, and the Epistles to Timothy, Titus and Philemon.* Trans. T. A. Small. Eds. David W. Torrance and Thomas F. Torrance. Vol. 10 (Grand Rapids, MI: Eerdmans, 1964), p. 330.

Some allege that such a view of Scripture amounts to 'bibliolatry', leading to the worship of a book rather than of God. But such an allegation presupposes that Scripture is something less than the word of God, for if 'what Scripture says' is equivalent to 'what God says', then Calvin's logic is flawless. We do indeed owe as much reverence to the Bible as we do to God himself.

How can it be otherwise since the Bible's claim for itself is abundantly clear? This explains why, for the apostles of the New Testament, 'the Bible says', or 'it says', or 'God says', ended all arguments (cf. Acts 13:34; Rom. 9:13, 15, 17). New Testament authors viewed the Old Testament as 'the oracles of God' (Rom. 3:2; cf. Acts 7:38; 1 Pet. 4:11; Heb. 5:12).

When is the Bible the word of God?

Third, 2 Timothy 3:16, 17 teaches that Scripture does not *become* the word (when we are moved to acknowledge it as such); Scripture *is* the word of God. Swiss theologian Karl Barth, who dominated much of twentieth-century theological thinking, believed that Scripture is a witness *to* divine revelation, but can never be God's word in any *static* sense – that is, words contained in a book.[1] He argued that the word of God is an 'event' – a divine act – when and where God pleases. Most often the event takes place when Scripture is being preached and proclaimed. In this view, the Bible and its proclamation are indirect channels through which the word of God emerges.

[1] 'The Christian Understanding of Revelation', Open Lectures given at Bonn University, summer 1947, in *Against the Stream: Shorter Post-War Writings*, ed. Ronald Gregor Smith (London: SCM Press, 1954), pp. 217ff.

The statements made in the preceding paragraph are, of course, as slippery as an eel; and in Barth's mind they are meant to be. According to this view, Scripture may witness *to* the word of God, and it may even be the channel through which the word of God emerges; but Scripture is not in itself the word of God. This view is dogmatically refuted by 2 Timothy 3:16, 17.

What Scripture is 'for'

Fourth, because Scripture is 'breathed out by God', it is always profitable. We will have more to say on this in the final chapter, but for now we shall note that Scripture is 'profitable ['useful' or 'beneficial'] for teaching, for reproof, for correction, and for training in righteousness'. The extent of its profitability is far-reaching and comprehensive:

• The Scriptures are profitable for *teaching*. The first application of Scripture concerns the mind – how and what we are to think. The Bible corrects false understanding and the idolatry that accompanies it. The mind – what we think and believe – matters a great deal.

• The Scriptures are profitable for *reproof*. They rebuke and correct at the point of our will, the seat of desire, motivation, and action. At the core of our being is the faculty of resolve and determination which must be harnessed and steered in a Godward and godly direction.

• The Scriptures are profitable for *correction*. Scripture sets right what is out of line. Possibly there is an appeal to the affections in the use of this word (a word found only here in the New Testament).

• The Scriptures are profitable for *training in righteousness*. This may involve *discipline*, as the use of the same word in Hebrews 12:7 suggests: 'It is for discipline that you have to endure. God is treating you as sons. For what son is there whom his father does not discipline?' Scripture addresses our overall lifestyle.

Self-authenticating

How can we be sure that the Bible is the word of God? One answer is that the Holy Spirit testifies to its authority (the so-called *internal testimony of the Holy Spirit*). We will examine this in fuller detail in chapter 7. But in addition to the witness of the Holy Spirit, there is the witness of Scripture itself. This passage of Scripture (2 Tim. 3:16, 17) testifies to the divine origin or source of Scripture. Scripture claims its origin to be from the mouth of God. In this way, Scripture authenticates itself.

And how could it be otherwise? If Scripture is indeed the divine word, what other testimony to its identity, higher than itself, could corroborate such a claim? This may sound like circular reasoning, and indeed, it is! It is of the nature of absolute claims to be circular. The *Westminster Confession of Faith* puts the matter boldly and starkly:

> The authority of the Holy Scripture, for which it ought to be believed, and obeyed, depends not upon the testimony of any man, or church; but wholly upon God (who is truth itself) the author thereof: and therefore it is to be received, because it is the word of God.[1]

[1] *Westminster Confession of Faith*, I:4.

And John Calvin, referring to this phenomenon, came to this conclusion:

> Let this point therefore stand: those whom the Holy Spirit has inwardly taught truly rest upon Scripture, and that Scripture indeed is self-authenticated; hence it is not right to subject it to proof and reasoning.[1]

What the Bible says, God says.

[1] John Calvin, *Institutes of the Christian Religion*, John T. McNeill, ed.; tr. Ford Lewis Battles (Philadelphia: Westminster Press, 1960), I.vii.5.

5

The Bible and Human Authorship (Part 1)

For no prophecy was ever produced by the will of man, but men spoke from God as they were carried along by the Holy Spirit. – 2 Peter 1:21

What exactly is the Bible? On one level, it is a collection of approximately three-quarters of a million words, in sixty-six books, originally written in three distinct languages (Hebrew, Aramaic, and Greek), over a period of a thousand years and more, by some forty different authors from a variety of cultures and settings, in an assortment of different genres, including history, prophecy, sermons, letters, formal covenant treaties, travel narratives, poetry, parables, proverbs, architectural instructions, apocalypses, gospels, laws (moral, civil, and ceremonial), inventories, and much more. To these various genres, distinctive rules of interpretation apply (history read as history, parable as parable, apocalypses as apocalypses, etc.), ensuring that a 'literal' interpretation means just that – interpretation that is sensitive to the *literary* genre.

Every word of the Bible in its original Hebrew, Aramaic, and Greek is the product of divine 'out-breathing' (2 Tim. 3:16). Strictly speaking, this attribution concerns the sacred writings of the Old Testament: every word of these scriptures is what God intended and therefore all Scripture is infallible and inerrant (totally true and entirely trustworthy). Concerning the New Testament, the apostle Peter adds a significant insight when he chastises 'the ignorant and unstable' for twisting Paul's letters 'to their own destruction, as they do *the other Scriptures*' (2 Pet. 3:16). The inference is clear and inescapable: Paul's letters are on a par with Holy Scripture and are to be regarded as such.

The Bible, then, is both 'from men' and 'from God' – something which Peter makes abundantly clear when he writes, '*men* spoke from God as they were carried along by the Holy Spirit' (2 Pet. 1:21). The human authorship of Scripture (what theologians have termed its *organic* nature) ensures that we may legitimately say 'Moses wrote' or 'John wrote', discerning individual stylistic features unique to individual authors.

The Bible and human agency

Scripture is both human *and* divine: totally human and totally divine in its origin. Consider the following verses:

> 'Then the LORD put out his hand and touched my mouth. And the LORD said to me, "Behold, I have put my words in your mouth"' (Jer. 1:9).

> 'Who through the mouth of our father David, your servant,

said by the Holy Spirit, "Why did the Gentiles rage, and the peoples plot in vain?"' (Acts 4:25).

'Therefore, as the Holy Spirit says, "Today, if you hear his voice"' (Heb. 3:7, citing Psa. 95:7-11).

'And the Holy Spirit also bears witness to us' (Heb. 10:15, citing Jer. 31:31).

'For the Scripture says to Pharaoh, "For this very purpose I have raised you up, that I might show my power in you, and that my name might be proclaimed in all the earth"' (Rom. 9:17; note that it is God who spoke these words to Pharaoh in Exod. 9:16. Scripture says = God says).

Men wrote the Bible – 'men spoke from God' – and whatever the precise nature of the divine agency at work in and through these men, the Scriptures came into being through human agency. These human authors included men of diverse educational and social backgrounds – think of Moses and his Egyptian education and upbringing, or Isaiah and Amos with their urban and rural backgrounds respectively. These writers also had differing temperaments – we need only think of how the Book of Kells[1] depicted the writers of the four Gospels by a winged man or angel (Matthew), a lion (Mark), an ox (Luke), and an eagle (John), which illustrates the diversity of the Bible's human authorship.

[1] The *Book of Kells* (or *Book of Columba*) is an illuminated manuscript in Latin which contains the four Gospels. It dates to around 800, and takes its name from the Abbey of Kells (Co. Meath, Ireland), which was its home for many centuries. It is on permanent display at Trinity College Library, Dublin.

Human authorship gives rise to stylistic distinctions. Bible readers have noted, for example, that Isaiah has a tendency to employ the ascription 'the Holy One of Israel' when speaking of God (it is used twenty-five times in Isaiah and only seven times in the rest of the Old Testament).[1]

Other examples include Jeremiah's tendency to introspection, giving way to subjective analyses of himself – one writer calls him 'the most human prophet'.[2] Or think of John's use of simple words in the prologue to his Gospel in order to express the profoundest truths. Or again, recall Paul's ability to employ lengthy sentences that, as one commentator puts it, 'are extended by relative and causal clauses and participial constructions'.[3]

Human authorship is also seen in the use of 'ordinary' sources of information. Thus, the Chronicler refers to accessing material from 'the Chronicles of Samuel the Seer' (1 Chron. 29:29).[4] And in a similar manner, Luke informs his readers of his research methodology:

> Inasmuch as many have undertaken to compile a narrative of the things that have been accomplished among us, just as those who from the beginning were eyewitnesses and ministers of the word have delivered them to us, it seemed

[1] Alec Motyer, *Isaiah*, Tyndale Old Testament Commentaries (Leicester: IVP, 1999), p. 26.

[2] John Skinner, *Prophecy and Religion* (London: Cambridge University Press, 1963), p. 350.

[3] Peter T. O'Brien, *The Letter to the Ephesians*, Pillar New Testament Commentary (Grand Rapids, MI: Eerdmans; Leicester: Apollos, 1999), p. 6.

[4] This may simply be a reference to the canonical books of 1 & 2 Samuel and 1 & 2 Kings.

> good to me also, having followed all things closely for some time past, to write an orderly account for you, most excellent Theophilus, that you may have certainty concerning the things you have been taught (Luke 1:1-4).

Similarly, observations have been made of the Bible authors' (*and* Author's) use of similar stylistic features that reflect 'secular' convention. Much has been written, for example, on the influence of Ancient Near Eastern literature on the Bible.[1] On the other end of the historical scale, we should recall that the New Testament writers were nearly all Jewish, reared in Jewish cultures, and (more than likely) that influenced how they thought, reasoned, and responded to various circumstances.

What have we said so far?

We can and do discern the input of individual authors (Bible writers) within the biblical canon – we have been able to note their personality, background, and research methodology, for example.

From this observation, another may be made: that individual authors contribute particular theological features and grow and advance their own analysis and arguments. Isaiah, as we have seen, advances our understanding of

[1] For a recent, conservative introduction, see John D. Currid, *Against the Gods: The Polemical Theology of the Old Testament* (Wheaton: IL: Crossway, 2013). See also Meredith Kline, *The Structure of Biblical Authority* (Grand Rapids, MI: Eerdmans, 1971); George E. Mendenhall, *Law and Covenant in Israel and the Ancient Near East* (Pittsburg: Biblical Colloquium, 1955). For a general introduction to this material, see Bill T. Arnold and Bryan E. Beyer, *Encountering the Old Testament: A Christian Survey* (Grand Rapids, MI: Baker Books, 1999), pp. 148-150.

holiness and, thereby, advances our understanding of the doctrine of God. Similarly, Hosea elaborates on the nature of covenant love. Ezekiel, from the vantage point of exile and the imminent destruction of Jerusalem and the temple, expands on the nature of God's glory. And in the New Testament, Paul (to limit ourselves to just one example) expands on the nature of justification and union with Christ. Indeed, the latter concept, as has often been pointed out, was surely derived from Paul's own participation in the death of Stephen; as he later discovered, in so far as he had persecuted Stephen, he had in fact been persecuting the Lord Jesus Christ (Acts 9:4; 22:7; 26:14).

The point here is that the revelation of God to man is not *flat* but *progressive*. God employed the authors of Scripture, with their unique personalities and backgrounds, to advance our understanding of his purpose and grace in the gospel. Furthermore, this advancement can be seen in the experience and understanding of the individual authors.

Some have been reticent to advance a robust doctrine of the human component of Scripture's origin ('*men* spoke', 2 Pet. 1:21) for fear that in doing so, Scripture might appear less 'inspired'. But this is a mistake. The fact is, Scripture is dual-authored. God wrote and men wrote. God wrote *through* human instruments. Obviously, this requires some explanation, something we will address in the next chapter.

6

The Bible and Human Authorship (Part 2)

How did God write Scripture *through* men? It would be an error to assume that the *mode* of inspiration was always dictation – the idea that Bible writers were employed simply as 'human typewriters'. However, there were occasions when Bible writers took dictation! The seven letters to the churches in Asia Minor found in Revelation 2 and 3, for example, are all prefaced by a command from the Lord Jesus to the apostle John: 'To the angel of the church in … *write*' (Rev. 2:1, 8, 12, 18; 3:1, 7, 14). Clearly, John took down exactly – word-for-word – what the Lord Jesus dictated to him. Similarly, the Ten Commandments are introduced with the formula: 'And God spoke all these words, saying …' (Exod. 20:1; cf. 'He [the LORD] said …' Deut. 5:5).

But Bible writers should not be viewed as mere secretaries. As we have seen, Luke tells us that his method was different, that is, he recorded interviews with eye-witnesses, checked his facts, engaged in meticulous historical research

(Luke 1:1-4). Occasionally, some allusions to the Old Testament Scriptures are made with surprising informality, for example, 'It has been testified somewhere ...' as though the author is relying on his 'fallible' memory (Heb. 2:6). But we should not draw from such allusions the conclusion that these quotations are somehow *less* inspired.

In addition, there appear to have been occasions when Bible writers wrote *beyond their own knowledge and understanding*. Peter, for example, writes:

> Concerning this salvation, the prophets who prophesied about the grace that was to be yours searched and inquired carefully, inquiring what person or time the Spirit of Christ in them was indicating when he predicted the sufferings of Christ and the subsequent glories (1 Pet. 1:10, 11).

Clearly, the prophets wrote about things they didn't fully grasp.

The relationship between human authors and divine authorship – 'God's words in men's mouths' – is not an easy one. We should not attempt to parcel out 'inspired bits' and 'uninspired bits' – a trend all too common among evangelicals, past and present.

Total, absolute sovereignty in human freedom

'No prophecy of Scripture comes from someone's own interpretation. For no prophecy was ever produced by the will of man, but men spoke from God as they were carried along by the Holy Spirit' (2 Pet. 1:20-21). Peter's choice of words is fascinating. Yes, *Peter's* choice as well as the *Holy*

Spirit's choice – the Holy Spirit superintending the human freedom of Peter.

Several points need to be made.

Firstly, what is the precise meaning of 'prophecy' here? Is it meant to allude simply to those specific prophecies about the coming of Christ (Peter has been alluding to the coming and transfiguration of Jesus), or is it a more general reference to the Old Testament in its entirety? Even if we were to limit the term to the writings of the prophets (rather than to the entirety of Scripture), the point being made is substantially the same: the prophetic writings are 'Scripture' and what is true about them is true *because* they are Scripture.

Secondly, the idea of inspiration is not applied to the writers. The writers are not breathed out by God or breathed into by God. Peter says that they were 'carried along' by the Holy Spirit. Without lessening the human involvement – their *conscious* participation – the point the text is making is that what the prophets wrote is what the Holy Spirit intended them to write, no more and no less.

Thirdly, the verb in verse 21, 'produced'[1] – 'no prophecy was ever *produced* by the will of man' – is also employed in verse 17, where it refers to the voice of the heavenly Father

[1] We are following the ESV text at this point which renders the Greek word *enegkō* as 'produced', suggesting that the issue at hand is a question as to the source of the prophecy. Other translations suggest the issue is one of false interpretation of prophecy, e.g. NRSV, 'no prophecy of scripture is a matter of one's own interpretation'. For a defence of the former view, see Gene L. Green, *Jude and 2 Peter*, Baker Exegetical Commentary on the New Testament (Grand Rapids, MI: Baker Books, 2008), p. 231.

that Jesus heard: 'the voice *was borne* to him by the Majestic Glory'. The English text hides the fact that Peter is making a dual point here: 'our author is clearly negating one source of prophecy and affirming another, which is heavenly, just as the voice which came to Jesus was heavenly'.[1]

Fourthly, the positive verb, 'carried along', is a very strong one. It is the verb employed by Luke to describe how the ship in which Paul and his captors sailed, when caught in a violent storm, was *driven along* by the wind (Acts 27:15, 17). The emphasis lies upon total sovereignty. These men are 'carried along' by the Holy Spirit. They are not simply prompted or led, but carried by him. The idea conveyed is one of superintendence and restraint. In a magisterial analysis of this verse (along with its companion verse in 2 Tim. 3:16, 17), American theologian B. B. Warfield (1851–1921) comments:

> The term used here is a very specific one. It is not to be confounded with guiding, or directing, or controlling, or even leading in the full sense of that word. It goes beyond all such terms, in assigning the effect produced specifically to the active agent. What is 'borne' is taken up by the 'bearer', and conveyed by the 'bearer's' power, not its own, to the 'bearer's' goal, not its own. The men who spoke from God are here declared, therefore, to have been taken up by the Holy Spirit and brought by his power to the goal of his choosing. The things which they spoke under this operation of the Spirit were therefore his things, not theirs.

[1] Peter H. Davids, *The Letters of 2 Peter and Jude*, Pillar New Testament Commentary (Grand Rapids, MI: Eerdmans, 2006), p. 213.

> And that is the reason which is assigned why 'the prophetic word' is so sure. Though spoken through the instrumentality of men, it is, by virtue of the fact that these men spoke 'as borne by the Holy Spirit', an immediately Divine word.[1]

And what is the result of this action by the Holy Spirit? That no Scripture is the product of human initiative alone:

- Scripture does not come 'from someone's own interpretation' (verse 20), and,
- Scripture is not 'produced by the will of man' (verse 21).

Care must be taken not to contradict what has already been said about the human involvement and initiative in the production of Scripture. Men wrote. And their contributions are discernible. But the finished product is what God intended. The nuance is breathtaking. Sovereignty and responsibility in perfect harmony.

Certainty

What, then, is Peter saying?

Firstly, he is making a declaration regarding *the adequacy of human language to convey divine truth*. Scripture declares 'God has spoken', employing words – verbs, nouns, adjectives, and grammatical constructions that convey truth, '*true* truth'. To doubt this (as many do) is to doubt the incarnation of Jesus Christ. For, when Jesus spoke, God spoke. The same is true, in no less a fashion, of the Bible. In the face of scepticism and doubt, to take

[1] B. B. Warfield, 'The Biblical Idea of Inspiration', in *The Inspiration and Authority of the Bible* (Philadelphia, PA: The Presbyterian and Reformed Publishing Company, 1970), p. 137.

up the Bible and read its words is to hear the very voice of God – not simply *through* the words in some form of 'mystical encounter', but *in* the very words themselves.[1]

Secondly, Peter is making a statement that *Scripture can be trusted on all matters to which it speaks, however incidental they may seem*. Thus, Scripture alludes to relatively minor historical incidents:

- The Queen of the South visited Solomon (Matt. 12:42; Luke 11:31-32).
- David ate the consecrated bread (Mark 2:25, 26).
- Moses lifted up the serpent in the desert (John 3:14).
- Abraham gave a tenth of the spoils to Melchizedek (Heb. 7:2).
- Eight people were saved in the ark (1 Pet. 3:20).
- Balaam's ass spoke (2 Pet. 2:16).

As New Testament scholar and prolific author D. A. Carson points out:

> One of the most intriguing examples is found on the lips of Jesus (Matt. 22:41-46; Mark 12:35-37). Jesus cites Psalm 110, which according to the superscription, is a psalm of David. The important thing to observe is that the validity of Jesus' argument here depends utterly on the assumption that the superscription is accurate. If the psalm were not written by David, then David did not speak of the Messiah as his Lord, while still referring to the 'my Lord' to whom 'the LORD' spoke. If, say, a courtier had composed the psalm then 'my Lord' could easily be understood to refer to David

[1] J. I. Packer's essay, 'The Adequacy of Human Language', is vital reading on this topic. See his *Collected Shorter Writings*, III:23-50.

himself, or to one of the monarchs who succeeded him (as many modern critics suppose).[1]

The point here is this: the Bible can be trusted on matters of 'relative unimportance', and therefore in its *details* as well as in its overall teaching. The trend today is to suggest that we should not be too concerned about the details. The problem with such a view is that it is impossible to gauge where inspiration ends and human fallibility begins.

The point of 2 Peter 1:19-21 is that *all* Scripture is 'from God'. Parcelling out parts that are inspired and parts that are not is entirely illegitimate. Some insist that the *organic* nature of Scripture must involve error since 'to err is human'.[2] But the reality is that, according to this line of argument, *all* Scripture is human and therefore subject to suspicion.

Thirdly, the Scriptures are *more certain and therefore more trustworthy than our experience*. The ESV renders 2 Peter 1:19 in this way, 'we have the prophetic word *more fully confirmed*'. This suggests that the point is one of *comparison*. This was hardly controversial in Peter's day for the current Jewish view was that prophecy was always more reliable than any vision or voice from heaven. Peter, then,

[1] D. A. Carson, *Collected Writings on Scripture* (Wheaton, IL: Crossway, 2010), pp. 25-26.

[2] As Sinclair B. Ferguson has pointed out: 'strictly speaking, "to err" is not so much human as it is fallen'. *From the Mouth of God: Trusting, Reading, and Applying the Bible* (Edinburgh: Banner of Truth Trust, 2014), p. 38. Man, as originally created by God, was perfect in knowledge, righteousness, and holiness. The human inclination 'to err' was one of the disastrous consequences of Adam's fall into sin.

seems to be saying that 'the prophetic Scriptures are surer than any experience I have to share, so I appeal to those Scriptures to confirm what I have told you'.[1]

Ultimately, the point he is making is that despite the incarnation ('the coming') and transfiguration of Jesus (2 Pet. 1:16), in addition to the voice of the heavenly Father that accompanied the latter, Scripture – 'the prophetic word' – is 'more fully confirmed' (verse 19). The physical and tangible realities of the incarnation and transfiguration add a note of confirmation to the prophetic word of Scripture. How important it is, then, to see how in this passage Peter draws the attention of the readers of his letter – not to the incarnation and transfiguration – *but to Scripture itself*. The ultimate source of certainty lies in the prophetic word of Scripture because it is 'from God' (2 Pet. 1:21).

And because Scripture is from God, we 'do well to pay attention' to what it says, not least because 'what Scripture says, God says' (2 Pet. 1:19). It is like 'a lamp shining in a dark place'. The word for 'dark place' occurs only here in the New Testament, but Peter may be thinking of Psalm 119:105, 'Your word is a lamp to my feet and a light to my path.' The 'prophetic word' is to be our guide 'until the day dawns and the morning star rises in [our] hearts' (2 Pet. 1:19). The Old Testament background to this vivid image is found in Balaam's final oracle:

> I see him, but not now;
> I behold him, but not near:

[1] J. I. Packer, *Truth and Power*, p. 223.

> a star shall come out of Jacob,
> and a sceptre shall rise out of Israel (Num. 24:17).

Following the night ('dark place') comes the light of a new day – in this case, the second coming of Christ and the dawning of the new heavens and new earth: 'But according to his promise we are waiting for new heavens and a new earth in which righteousness dwells' (2 Pet. 3:13). When the morning star appears, a new age will dawn – something which Isaiah had prophesied (Isa. 65:17; 66:22) – and there will be no further need of Scripture. The rising of Christ in our hearts will give us full knowledge: 'As for prophecies, they will pass away; as for tongues, they will cease; as for knowledge, it will pass away. For we know in part and we prophesy in part, but when the perfect comes, the partial will pass away' (1 Cor. 13:8-10).[1]

The point, then, is that we will do well to pay attention to Scripture as a lamp that shines in a dark place anticipating the dawn and rising of the morning star in our hearts. The Scriptures (the Old Testament Scriptures in this case!) anticipated the coming of Christ – in his fullness and glory, both his first and second coming. And as we traverse this interim between the 'now' and the 'not yet', we will do well to counter unbelief and uncertainty by ensuring that the Scriptures occupy a central and foundational place in our

[1] The 'perfect' in these verses may also refer to the closing of the canon of the New Testament, rather than the return of Christ. See Sinclair B. Ferguson, *The Holy Spirit*, pp. 226-228. For the view that it refers to the second coming of Christ (Gk. *parousia*), see Richard B. Gaffin, *Perspectives on Pentecost* (1979; repr. Phillipsburg, NJ: Presbyterian and Reformed, 1993).

minds and hearts. 'Grow in the grace and knowledge of our Lord and Saviour Jesus Christ', Peter tells his readers (2 Pet. 3:18). How are we to grow? What has been given to us to enable us to advance in our walk with Jesus Christ? *Scripture!* That is what we have, and that is all we need. Scripture given. Scripture interpreted by the help of the Holy Spirit. Scripture hidden and treasured in our hearts. Scripture obeyed in all its warnings and exhortations. For when we read Scripture, it is the voice of God that speaks in every word of it.

Pay attention to the written word of God!

7

The Bible and the Testimony of the Holy Spirit

While they were talking and discussing together, Jesus himself drew near and went with them. – Luke 24:15

In a fascinating use of the present tense, the author of Hebrews writes of the way in which our heavenly Father is always communicating with us in the Bible: 'And have you forgotten the exhortation that *addresses* you as sons?' (Heb. 12:5). Every time we read the Bible, God is speaking to us. He wants us to pay attention, understand, and respond to what he is saying. It is by the ministry of the Holy Spirit through the written word of Scripture that this communication takes place.

At the end of chapter 4, we encountered briefly the way in which the Bible *authenticates itself*. In addition, we drew attention to the witness of the Holy Spirit to the Bible's divine origin and consequent trustworthiness. We need to return to these issues and address them more fully.

When God speaks, he does so through the Holy Spirit. Several passages in Acts make this clear:

> In those days Peter stood up among the brothers (the company of persons was in all about 120) and said, 'Brothers, the Scripture had to be fulfilled, which the Holy Spirit spoke beforehand by the mouth of David concerning Judas, who became a guide to those who arrested Jesus' (Acts 1:15, 16).

> And when they heard it, they lifted their voices together to God and said, 'Sovereign Lord, who made the heaven and the earth and the sea and everything in them, who through the mouth of our father David, your servant, said by the Holy Spirit ...' (Acts 4:24, 25).

> The Holy Spirit was right in saying to your fathers through Isaiah the prophet ... (Acts 28:25).[1]

Father, Son and Holy Spirit

These passages clearly indicate that the New Testament writers understood that the mind of the Holy Spirit and what is written in the pages of Scripture are one and the same. Similarly, in our previous chapter, we saw how the divine and human authorship of Scripture are to be understood concurrently. The Holy Spirit speaks through human agents. This is what Jesus promised to his disciples in the Upper Room:

> When the Spirit of truth comes, he will guide you into all the truth, for he will not speak on his own authority, but whatever he hears he will speak, and he will declare to you

[1] Similar statements can be found in Heb. 3:7, 8; 9:7, 8; 10:15-17.

> the things that are to come. He will glorify me, for he will take what is mine and declare it to you. All that the Father has is mine; therefore I said that he will take what is mine and declare it to you (John 16:13-15).

The apostles received three promises from Jesus: (1) they will *remember* Jesus' words; (2) they will *understand* Jesus' words; and (3) they will *receive revelation* about the future.

Notice the trinitarian nature of this process: the Father speaks to the Son, and the Holy Spirit receives from the Son and gives to the apostles.

Notice also how this process becomes the subject matter of Jesus' prayer recorded in John 17. Having received the word from his Father (John 17:7, 8), Jesus now gives that word to his apostles (John 17:14), who will in turn take it to others (John 17:20).

The Holy Spirit gave us Scripture through his servants: 'men spoke from God as they were carried along by the Holy Spirit' (2 Pet. 1:21).

The Spirit also enables us to *receive* the Scriptures as the word of God. Resistant as we are by nature, only the Holy Spirit can enable us to discern Scripture's true meaning: 'The natural person does not accept the things of the Spirit of God, for they are folly to him, and he is not able to understand them because they are spiritually discerned' (1 Cor. 2:14).

Illumination

This is precisely what the Thessalonians experienced. They 'received the word of God ... [and] accepted it not as the word of men but as what it really is, the word of God' (1 Thess. 2:13). How so? Because of the role of the Holy Spirit. The gospel first came to them, 'not only in word, but also in power and in the Holy Spirit and with full conviction' (1 Thess. 1:5).

Just as Jesus 'opened' the minds of the two disciples whom he met on the road to Emmaus 'to understand the Scriptures' (Luke 24:45), so he continues this ministry through 'another Helper' (John 14:16) – the Holy Spirit. It is as though, when we read the Scriptures, the Bible 'comes alive'.

This ministry of the Holy Spirit has been referred to as the internal testimony of the Holy Spirit. It was an important emphasis in the sixteenth-century Reformation. It was John Calvin who drew special attention to the role of the Holy Spirit in confirming to us the authenticity of Scripture.

> The highest proof of Scripture derives in general from the fact that God in person speaks in it … We ought to seek our conviction in a higher place than human reasons, judgments, or conjectures, that is, in the secret testimony of the Holy Spirit. The testimony of the Spirit is more excellent than all reason. For as God alone is a fit witness of himself in his word, so also the word will not find acceptance in men's hearts before it is sealed by the inward testimony of the Spirit. The same Spirit, therefore, who has spoken through the mouths of the prophets must penetrate into our hearts to persuade us that they faithfully proclaimed what had been divinely commanded. Isaiah very aptly expresses this connection in these words: 'My Spirit which

> is in you, and the words that I have put in your mouth, and the mouths of your offspring, shall never fail' (Isa. 59:21). Some good folk are annoyed that a clear proof is not ready at hand when the impious, unpunished, murmur against God's word. As if the Spirit were not called both 'seal' and 'guarantee' (2 Cor. 1:22) for confirming the faith of the godly; because until he illumines their minds, they ever waver among many doubts![1]

The witness of the Spirit does not occur apart from the word of God but concurrently with it. As the apostle John writes:

> But you have been anointed by the Holy One, and you all have knowledge. I write to you, not because you do not know the truth, but because you know it, and because no lie is of the truth (1 John 2:20, 21).

John is alluding to the fact that Christians are in possession of the Holy Spirit who invests believers with discernment, wisdom and a witness to the authenticity of the Scriptures.

Come, Holy Spirit

A practical conclusion seems necessary in order to fully grasp the importance of the witness of the Holy Spirit in advancing our understanding of, and profit to be gained from, Scripture. We ought to be diligent in praying to our heavenly Father that, together with the Son, he might send the Holy Spirit in his fullness to illuminate our otherwise darkened minds as we diligently search the Scriptures.

[1] John Calvin, *Institutes*, I.vii.4.

Without the Spirit's ministry, our activities in the Scriptures will profit us nothing. This is how our heavenly Father ministers to us, by sending forth his Holy Spirit into our hearts. This is how Jesus draws near to us, by sending his representative Agent and Helper to aid us to see and appreciate the things that belong to him (as he did himself and in person with the two disciples on the way to Emmaus).

Praying for the Holy Spirit before reading and studying Scripture is a vital and necessary mark of true discipleship. Without the Spirit, Scripture will profit us nothing.

8

The Canon of Scripture

And count the patience of our Lord as salvation, just as our beloved brother Paul also wrote to you according to the wisdom given him, as he does in all his letters when he speaks in them of these matters. There are some things in them that are hard to understand, which the ignorant and unstable twist to their own destruction, as they do the other Scriptures.

—2 Peter 3:15, 16

'Canon' is a Greek word (*kanōn*). Originally, it was used for a reed, a standard device for measurement. It therefore served to denote a rule or a fixed standard of measurement.[1] In this chapter, the term *canon* refers to the precise number and identity of the individual books of the Old and New Testaments. Given the ambiguity that surrounded seventeenth-century discussions of this issue, particularly with representatives of the Roman Catholic

[1] It is used this way in Gal. 6:16, 'And as for all who walk by this *rule* [*kanōn*] ...' The 'rule' in view is that mentioned at the close of the previous verse – the 'new creation' brought about by the coming of Christ.

Church and its use of Apocryphal writings,[1] the compilers of the Westminster Confession of Faith thought it necessary to include a list of the thirty-nine books of the Old Testament and the twenty-seven books of the New.[2]

In our time, much uncertainty exists over the issue of canon, mainly due to the recent publication of alternative Gospels 'written', it is argued, by figures such as Mary, Thomas, Philip, and even Judas.[3] The publication of '*Lost Scriptures*' – the title of one book purporting to have rediscovered 'Scriptures' otherwise lost or discarded[4] – creates the suspicion that the entire formation of the canon was the consequence of historical accidents and prejudice. Indeed, conservative scholars have long since spoken of the issue

[1] The 'Apocryphal writings' referred to here are a number of texts which were included in the Latin Vulgate and ancient Greek translation of the OT known as the Septuagint, but not in the Hebrew Bible (i.e. Old Testament). While Catholic tradition considers the texts to be deuterocanonical (belonging to a second canon), Protestants consider them apocryphal (of unknown authorship or of doubtful origin). This is why Protestant Bibles do not include the books within the Old Testament. However, some editions of the Bible have included them in a separate section.

[2] Chapter 1, section 2. Section 3 of the Confession specifically denies the canonicity of certain other books commonly found in *The Apocrypha*.

[3] On these publications and the issue of canon in general, see the definitive and highly recommended volumes by Michael J. Kruger, *Canon Revisited: Establishing the Origins and Authority of the New Testament Books* (Wheaton, IL: Crossway, 2012); *The Question of Canon: Challenging the Status Quo in the New Testament Debate* (Downers Grove, IL: IVP Academic, 2013).

[4] Bart D. Ehrman, *Lost Scriptures: Books That Did Not Make It into the New Testament* (Oxford: Oxford University Press, 2005). Readers should consult the following video by Michael J. Kruger in response to Bart Ehrman: *http://www.youtube.com/watch?v=A8sxmklrHMY&list=-PL56A66CB81EAAB1BC&index=3&feature=plpp_video.*

as 'the hidden, dragging illness of the church'.[1] The subject of 'canon' is a continuing source of discussion and debate.

Before we examine the merits or otherwise of additional New Testament books, we need to examine the canon of the Old Testament. The Old Testament canon is a much clearer issue and, in the end, the question of whether we accept it or not boils down to the matter of obedience to the Lord Jesus Christ. There can be no doubt that the Lord Jesus accepted the canon as we know it – the same books, though in the *order* of the Hebrew Scriptures, which is a different order from that found in traditional copies of the English Bible.

The Old Testament canon

The idea of canon – a fixed set of documents which God's people recognize as the authoritative word of God – is seen in the transition of rule from Moses to Joshua. As Exodus 24:3-8, Deuteronomy 31:9-13, and Joshua 1:7-9 make clear, God gave to the Israelites at that time not only a new leader (Joshua) but also the 'Book of the Covenant' (Exod. 24:7; cf. 2 Kings 23:2, 3, 21), or the 'Book of the Law' (Deut. 29:21; 31:26; Josh. 1:7) to which both the Israelites and Joshua were to yield obedience. This 'book' (in written form) was placed in the ark of the covenant (Deut. 31:26). The history of the Old Testament is described in terms of the people's obedience or disobedience to this Book of the Covenant.

[1] Herman Ridderbos, 'The Canon of the New Testament', *Revelation and the Bible: Contemporary Evangelical Thought*, ed. C. F. H. Henry (Grand Rapids, MI: Baker, 1958), p. 198.

The era of the Prophets expands and explains what is essentially contained in the book of the Law.

As we saw in chapter 3, the revelation of God is progressive and cumulative, and the contents of the Old Testament Scriptures grew. To 'the Law' (*Torah*, the five books of Moses) and 'the Prophets' (*Navi'im*) were added 'the Writings' (*Ketuvim*).[1] In this way, the books of Joshua, Judges, Samuel, and Kings are viewed as comprising the (Former) Prophets, while books such as Psalms, Proverbs, Job, Song of Solomon, Ruth, Lamentations, Ecclesiastes, Esther, Daniel, Nehemiah–Ezra, and Chronicles are included in the third part of the Hebrew Bible, 'the Writings'. Thus, the Hebrew Bible ends with Chronicles rather than Malachi. Also, the books of the Hebrew canon number twenty-four (as opposed to thirty-nine), because the Twelve Minor Prophets are reckoned as one book. The books of 1 and 2 Samuel, 1 and 2 Kings, 1 and 2 Chronicles and Ezra–Nehemiah are also considered single volumes, for they tell essentially one continuous story.

The exact history surrounding how and when individual books were viewed as canonical is complicated and in some aspects unknown. No credit should be given to the claim (sometimes made) that the Old Testament canon was 'fixed' at the Council of Jamnia in AD 90. The canon was viewed as fixed in Jesus' time.

And it is this factor – *how did Jesus and the New Testament writers view the Old Testament canon?* – that

[1] Combining the first letter of these three sections, the Hebrew Bible is often referred to as the *Tanakh*.

must prove decisive for us. Several matters must be considered:

- The way Old Testament quotations are introduced by 'it is written' (one word in Greek, *gegraptai*, John 6:31; 8:17; 12:14; etc.). In the words of Dutch theologian and biblical scholar Herman Ridderbos (1909–2007), it is a phrase which 'in the New Testament puts an end to all contradiction.'[1] Implicit in the use of the phrase is the idea of a fixed authoritative rule or canon.
- Decisive (as we saw at the close of chapter 2) was the way in which Jesus saw his own ministry as a fulfilment of the precise expectation of the Old Testament. His life and death were in fulfilment of that which had been written (Matt. 26:24; Mark 14:27; John 13:18; 15:25; etc.). The Old Testament canon, as received in Jesus' time, had absolute authority over his words and actions. There simply was no dispute over the content of the Old Testament canon.

It is indisputable that Jesus recognized the Hebrew Bible as canonical. For us to question the Old Testament's canonicity poses massive and fatal issues regarding our allegiance to the Lord Jesus Christ. How can we possibly worship him as our Lord and God (as Thomas did, cf. John 20:28) if he was wrong about the nature and content of the Old Testament? That perspective alone ends all discussion. Failure to end the discussion leads into some other religion, one that is decidedly not Christianity.

[1] Herman Ridderbos, *Studies in Scripture and Authority* (Grand Rapids, MI: Eerdmans, 1978), p. 21.

The New Testament canon

But what about the New Testament canon? Would John, or Matthew, or Paul be astonished if they knew that their writings were still being read in churches today? They might indeed be astonished that their writings were printed in books and are now available in digital format. But the New Testament authors believed that their writings were on a par with 'Scripture' (the Old Testament, i.e., the Hebrew Bible), and that their writings were intended for a wider audience than simply 'their first readers' (whoever they may have been).

Consider the following factors:

- Note that John echoes the phrase 'it is written' when he completes his own Gospel: 'but these are written so that you may believe that Jesus is the Christ, the Son of God, and that by believing you may have life in his name' (John 20:31). The phrase signifies complete authority and finality when used of the Old Testament, and John appears to be giving his own Gospel equal authority.
- Paul reminds Christians at Thessalonica that when he taught them it was nothing other and no less than 'the word of God' which they received from him (1 Thess. 2:13).
- Disobedience to the teaching in Paul's letters could lead to excommunication from the church: 'If anyone does not obey what we say in this letter, take note of that person, and have nothing to do with him, that he may be ashamed' (2 Thess. 3:14). Clearly, Paul's estimation of its contents exceeds mere advice and information.

• Apostolic letters were read alongside Old Testament Scripture: 'And when this letter has been read among you, have it also read in the church of the Laodiceans; and see that you also read the letter from Laodicea.' (Col. 4:16; cf. 1 Cor. 10:11 in which there is reference to the events of Old Testament history. These things were 'written down' for the instruction of the members of the Christian church living between the first and second advents of Christ – 'for our instruction, on whom the end of the ages has come.')

• The closing words of the book of Revelation add to the sense of John's estimation of its canonical nature: 'I warn everyone who hears the words of the prophecy of this book: if anyone adds to them, God will add to him the plagues described in this book, and if anyone takes away from the words of the book of this prophecy, God will take away his share in the tree of life and in the holy city, which are described in this book' (Rev. 22:18, 19).

• Note the way 1 Timothy 5:18 cites both Old and New Testament books (Deut. 25:4 and Luke 10:7) prefaced by the words, 'for the Scripture says'.

• And Peter clearly thinks of Paul's letters as Scripture: 'just as our beloved brother Paul also wrote to you according to the wisdom given him, as he does in all his letters when he speaks in them of these matters. There are some things in them that are hard to understand, which the ignorant and unstable twist to their own destruction, as they do the other Scriptures' (2 Pet. 3:15, 16).

The New Testament authors, therefore, perceived that they were writing on a level and with the same consequent authority as the Old Testament canon.

The role of a New Testament apostle

Reading what Paul and the other apostles claim about their writings makes us ask, where did such confidence in their own significance come from? Were they simply arrogant, filled with a sense of their own self-importance? No! They were 'appointed' and 'named' *apostles* by the Lord Jesus Christ, and they were well aware of the nature of their unique office.

But what exactly was an apostle? Briefly, an apostle was someone given authority to speak on another's behalf. Apostles such as Peter and Paul were *sub*-apostles of *the* Apostle – Jesus Christ ('the apostle and high priest of our confession', Heb. 3:1). The New Testament apostles spoke on behalf of Jesus. He chose them and gave them authority (Mark 3:13ff.). This explains Paul's robust defence of his apostleship in 1 Corinthians 9 and Galatians 1. There was more at stake than merely his own reputation. He was God's spokesman, God's ambassador: to deny him was to deny God. Apostles received their commission from Christ himself (Gal. 1:11, 12).

Emerging New Testament canon

The early church traversed a very fluid time without the help of a fixed New Testament canon. It took time for all the churches to have access to all twenty-seven books which were recognized as canonical. Many Christians in the first century, for example, simply had no access whatsoever to large sections of the New Testament. Imagine the difficulty involved in making and disseminating handwritten copies of these books! But by the end of the second century, the early church father Irenaeus of Lyon (*c.* AD 120–*c.* 200) tells us that almost all the New Testament books had been received as Scripture. And by the fourth century, all twenty-seven books were recognized as such.[1]

Debates occurred over the difficulty of certain books – the peculiarity of the style in Revelation, or James' stress on works which 'seemed' at odds with Paul's emphasis on 'faith alone apart from works' in his letter to the Galatians. The early Luther made a remark about the letter of James as a 'right epistle of straw', but he did not question its canonicity as is often assumed.

The canon of the Scripture was never something 'decided' by church leaders or in church councils. The canonicity of Scripture was rather recognized and affirmed because in these books God spoke as in no other writings. Reading some of the 'lost' Gospels, for example, will immediately demonstrate just how bizarre they are. Extravagant claims about their value are made from ignorance of their contents. Those who read them initially dismissed them. There are good reasons why they were 'lost'.

[1] In the East, the recognition of the New Testament canon is associated with the Thirty-ninth Paschal Letter of Athanasius in AD 367, and, in the West, it is associated with the Council of Carthage in AD 397.

9

The Bible and Inerrancy

Scripture cannot be broken. – John 10:35

The word *inerrancy* when used in relation to the Scriptures of the Old and New Testaments means that there are no errors in the Bible. The Bible is perfect. In the past, the word *infallible* was also used to describe the perfection of Scripture. Technically, infallibility refers to the Bible's *trustworthiness*. Inerrancy is a more precise term, claiming that the Bible *contains no mistakes*.

Inerrancy is a claim about the truthfulness of Scripture. When we say that the Bible is true, what exactly do we mean?

The transmission of Scripture

First, we do not mean that the Bible contains *all* truth. Consider the following:

- The relation between energy (E) and mass (m) may be formulated $E=mc^2$, where c is the speed of light.
- The chemical formula for Benzene is C_6H_6.

• The fourth symphony by Anton Bruckner (1824–96) is in the key of E-flat major.

• Sir Winston Leonard Spencer-Churchill, KG, OM, CH, TD, PC, DL, FRS, Hon. RA was born on November 30, 1874.

All these statements are true, but they are not found in Scripture.

Second, we do not mean that the Bible contains all *religious* truth. God reveals only what we need to know. 'The secret things belong to the LORD our God, but the things that are revealed belong to us and to our children' (Deut. 29:29).

Third, when we claim that the Bible is true and inerrant we mean that the Bible is *a perfect rule of faith and life*. It is adequate for doctrine (teaching us what we should know and believe), experience (teaching us how to respond emotionally to God's self-disclosure), ethics (teaching us how we should behave), and worship (informing us how we should praise God, individually and corporately).

In this way, the Bible is different from a creed or a confession of faith. The latter are 'subordinate standards'. Specifically, creeds and confessions are subordinate to Scripture. Creeds and confessions can be corrected and improved, whereas the Scriptures cannot. Because the Bible is God speaking, the Bible has the power to bind or set free the conscience.

Fourth, strictly speaking, the perfection of Scripture applies only to the *original* manuscripts of the Old and New Testaments, which respecting the Old Testament were written in Hebrew and Aramaic, and respecting the New

Testament were written in Greek. The Bible as we possess it consists of transmitted and translated copies. No original text of any single part of Scripture exists.

Before overreacting to the previous statement, we should be clear as to the implications of such statements of fact. We should bear in mind, for example, that we do not possess an original copy of Plato's *Republic* or Shakespeare's *Hamlet*. And yet, a great deal of confidence exists as to the authenticity of the copies that we do have in our possession.

Some might think that a statement concerning the inerrancy of documents that no longer exist seems practically meaningless. But such is not the case. Rigorous scientific methods are employed to examine all possible copies and to conclude the wording of the original text. Some of these copies are mere fragments of verses included in other writings and books. As these documents are compared and 'weighed' as to their relative importance, variations in transmission may be identified and analysed according to precise, scientific rules. Variations in transmission include the following examples:

- *Dittography* – Writing twice what should have been written only once. An example would be writing 'latter' instead of 'later'. 'Latter' means nearest the end. 'Later' means after something else.
- *Haplography* – The opposite of dittography. Writing once what should have been written twice. An example would be 'later' instead of 'latter'.
- *Fission* – Improperly dividing one word into two

words. An example would be changing 'nowhere' into 'now here'.

• *Fusion* – Combining the last letter of one word with the first letter of the next word. An example would be changing 'Look it is there in the cabinet' to 'Look it is therein the cabinet.'

• *Homophony* – Writing a word with a different meaning for another word when both words have the exact same pronunciation. 'Meat' and 'meet', for example. Or the grammarian's favourite, 'their' and 'there'.

• *Metathesis* – An improper exchange in the order of letters. Examples would be 'mast' in place of 'mats', or 'cast' in place of 'cats'.

None of this should alarm us unduly. Consider the chart on the next page. It demonstrates that the degree of confidence in discovering the original text of Scripture is monumentally more assured than for some of the classic texts of Greek literature. In fact, of the 150,000 identified variants in the available texts of Scripture, 99% of them have no significance whatsoever.

Translation

Fifth, the inerrancy of Scripture is not a statement about any one particular translation of the Bible. Before we examine the important issue of translation, we should recall that the translation of Scripture into the common language of the nations cost people their lives. William Tyndale, for example, was executed in August 1536 for translating the Bible into English.

Author	When Written	Earliest Copy	Time Span	Number of Copies/or Partial Copies
Homer (*Iliad*)	900 BC	400 BC	500 years	643
Caesar (*The Gallic Wars*)	100 - 44 BC	900 AD	1,000 years	10
Plato (*Tetralogies*)	427 - 347 BC	900 AD	1,200 years	7
Aristotle	384 - 322 BC	1,100 AD	1,400 years	49
Herodotus (*History*)	480 - 425 BC	900 AD	1,300 years	8
Euripides	480 - 406 BC	1,100 AD	1,500 years	9
New Testament	50 - 90 AD	130 AD	40 years	24,000

The work of translation from one language into another involves a precise philosophy and understanding of how accurate (*literal*) or free (*dynamic*) the resulting translation needs to be. If, for example, the original text is viewed as inerrant, the translation (it is argued) needs to reflect the original as much as is technically possible. Debate exists as to whether a literal and exact translation is ever achievable. Sometimes, single words in the original text require more than one word in a translation to convey their meaning.

The English Standard Version, for example, claims to be an 'essentially literal' translation. Other translations claim merely to provide a 'dynamic equivalent' rendition, arguing that total correspondence is not achievable or desirable if the result is a wooden and stilted text.

An interesting example is the translation of Philippians 2:7. Earlier versions of the ESV read that Jesus Christ 'made himself nothing'. More recent editions of the ESV have a literal translation, 'emptied himself'. The problem with using the verb 'to empty' as the literal equivalent of the Greek (*ekenōsen*) is providing an answer to the question, 'emptied himself *of what*?' Any answer to this question will involve a statement of heresy. Indeed, an errant movement in nineteenth-century Britain and Germany (known as *Kenoticism*) advocated that Jesus, in becoming a man, divested himself of aspects of his divine nature. For a while, some reticence existed in supplying a *literal* translation of Philippians 2:7. In failing to provide such a literal translation, the ESV was viewed by some to be employing double standards, criticizing the philosophy of *dynamic* equivalence on the one hand, while employing it on the other. The business of translation is a difficult one.

The importance of the doctrine of inerrancy

Church historian and author Steve Nichols gives the following account of an event that had significant repercussions on how the inerrancy of Scripture would be viewed in the years that followed, and why it has become an important issue in our time:

> The national meeting of the Southern Baptist Convention[1] [took place] in Pittsburgh [in 1983]. The convention began with a pastors' conference. The previous fall, in the suburbs of Chicago, seven people died having taken Tylenol laced with cyanide. It set off a national panic. One speaker at the pastors' conference took out a bottle of Tylenol and said, 'If I knew there was one capsule in this bottle that was laced with cyanide, I would throw the whole bottle out.' Then he picked up the Bible and said, 'If I knew there was one error in this book, I would throw the whole thing out.'[2]

Does it matter if the Bible is *errant* or *inerrant*, *fallible* or *infallible*? The *Chicago Statement on Biblical Inerrancy*[3] states:

[1] The Southern Baptist Convention is the world's largest Baptist denomination and the largest Protestant denomination in the USA.

[2] Stephen J. Nichols and Eric T. Brandt, eds., *Ancient Word, Changing Worlds: The Doctrine of Scripture* (Wheaton, IL: Crossway, 2009), p. 64.

[3] The *Chicago Statement on Biblical Inerrrancy* was the result of a conference sponsored by the International Council on Biblical Inerrancy (ICBI) and held in Chicago in October 1978, and attended by more than 200 evangelical leaders. The statement consists of 19 articles; each includes an affirmation and a denial, plus an extended 'explanation'. See http://library.dts.edu/Pages/TL/Special/ICBI_1.pdf for a copy of the statement.

> **We affirm** that a confession of the full authority, infallibility and inerrancy of Scripture is vital to a sound understanding of the whole of the Christian faith. We further affirm that such confession should lead to increasing conformity to the image of Christ.
>
> **We deny** that such confession is necessary for salvation. However, we further deny that inerrancy can be rejected without grave consequences both to the individual and to the church.

The statement strikes a delicate balance. On the one hand, it affirms that the doctrine of inerrancy is 'vital to a sound understanding of the whole of the Christian faith' and that to deny it has grave consequences for the individual and the church. However, this statement also makes clear that belief in inerrancy is not necessary for salvation.

That said, inerrancy is what Jesus believed. Responding to certain Jews who were attempting to stone him for blasphemy, Jesus argued a point from the book of Psalms, adding, almost as an aside, a most vitally important statement of fact: 'Scripture cannot be broken' (John 10:35). The verb Jesus employed is one that suggests being 'torn apart'. Such is the inner consistency of Scripture that it is impossible to set one scripture against another. And that inner coherence stems from one simple fact: the ultimate author of the Bible is God.

10

The Clarity or Perspicuity of Scripture

Now an angel of the Lord said to Philip, 'Rise and go toward the south to the road that goes down from Jerusalem to Gaza.' This is a desert place. And he rose and went. And there was an Ethiopian, a eunuch, a court official of Candace, queen of the Ethiopians, who was in charge of all her treasure. He had come to Jerusalem to worship and was returning, seated in his chariot, and he was reading the prophet Isaiah. And the Spirit said to Philip, 'Go over and join this chariot.' So Philip ran to him and heard him reading Isaiah the prophet and asked, 'Do you understand what you are reading?' And he said, 'How can I, unless someone guides me?' And he invited Philip to come up and sit with him. Now the passage of the Scripture that he was reading was this:

'Like a sheep he was led to the slaughter
and like a lamb before its shearer is silent,
so he opens not his mouth.

> *In his humiliation justice was denied him.*
> *Who can describe his generation?*
> *For his life is taken away from the earth.'*

> *And the eunuch said to Philip, 'About whom, I ask you, does the prophet say this, about himself or about someone else?' Then Philip opened his mouth, and beginning with this Scripture he told him the good news about Jesus. And as they were going along the road they came to some water, and the eunuch said, 'See, here is water! What prevents me from being baptized?' And he commanded the chariot to stop, and they both went down into the water, Philip and the eunuch, and he baptized him. And when they came up out of the water, the Spirit of the Lord carried Philip away, and the eunuch saw him no more, and went on his way rejoicing. But Philip found himself at Azotus, and as he passed through he preached the gospel to all the towns until he came to Caesarea.* – Acts 8:26-40

Can *anyone* read the Bible and understand its meaning? The question is more difficult to answer than one might think. Let us assume that the person can read and that the Bible is available in that person's native language. These assumptions should cause us to ponder what, in fact, was the case in the long dark years of the medieval period in Europe. Bibles were available only in Latin (a language only the well-educated understood), and were not for public reading. One only has to think of the opposition faced by such men as John Wycliffe of England (*c.* 1330–84), Jan Hus of Bohemia (1369–1415), and William Tyndale (1494–1536), to appreciate how difficult and costly it was going to be to place the Bible into the hands of the 'man in the street'.

For reasons that need not concern us here, the medieval Roman Catholic Church thought it necessary to prevent the general public from reading and interpreting the Scriptures without the aid of the church authorities. The 'ordinary' person could not be trusted to read the Bible unaided. Interpretation of the Scriptures was viewed as belonging exclusively to the pope, or the bishops sitting in properly authorized councils of the church. The individual was denied the right to read and study the Bible without the guidance of the church to interpret what was read.

The Reformation of the sixteenth century was to change all that. The great German reformer Martin Luther (1483–1546), defending the doctrine of the clarity of Scripture, wrote:

> You see, then, that the entire content of the Scriptures has now been brought to light, even though some passages which contain unknown words remain obscure. Thus it is unintelligent, and ungodly too, when you know that the contents of Scripture are as clear as can be, to pronounce them obscure on account of those few obscure words. If words are obscure in one place, they are clear in another. What God has so plainly declared to the world is in some parts of Scripture stated in plain words, while in other parts it still lies hidden under obscure words. But when something stands in broad daylight, and a mass of evidence

> for it is in broad daylight also, it does not matter whether there is any evidence for it in the dark. Who will maintain that the town fountain does not stand in the light because the people down some alley cannot see it, while everyone in the square can see it?[1]

And the *Westminster Confession of Faith* made a very clear statement on the essential clarity of Scripture in these words:

> All things in Scripture are not alike plain in themselves, nor alike clear unto all: yet those things which are necessary to be known, believed, and observed for salvation are so clearly propounded, and opened in some place of Scripture or other, that not only the learned, but the unlearned, in a due use of the ordinary means, may attain unto a sufficient understanding of them.[2]

The doctrine that insists that ordinary men and women may read the Bible and gain a sufficient understanding of its contents is called the *perspicuity* of Scripture. But what exactly do we mean by the 'perspicuity', or 'clarity', of Scripture?

First, *the Bible testifies to its own clarity.* The 'law of the LORD' 'enlightened the eyes' and was a 'lamp' to the feet and a 'light' to the path for the people of God (Psa. 19:8; 119:105). They were expected and encouraged to read and obey it, and were held accountable for all forms of non-compliance

[1] Martin Luther, *Bondage of the Will*, tr. J. I. Packer & O. R. Johnston (Grand Rapids: Fleming H. Revell, 1957), p. 72.

[2] *Westminster Confession of Faith*, I:7.

and disobedience. The Bible's inspiration – its 'breathed-out-ness' by God – makes it 'profitable ... for training in righteousness' (2 Tim. 3:16). The Bible does not portray itself as a book of secrets and codes requiring expert cryptographers to interpret it. John wrote his Gospel so that his readers might understand and believe, and that by believing they might 'have life' in Christ's name (John 20:31).

Second, *the perspicuity of Scripture does not mean that all of Scripture is equally clear to everyone.* Jesus specifically spoke in parables in order that some (those intent on maliciously using his words to spread discord) might not understand what he was saying (Mark 4:11, 12). And Peter confessed that there were 'some things' in Paul's letters that he found 'hard to understand' (2 Pet. 3:15, 16). Without considerable help from 'experts' ('skilled' and 'learned' men like Ezra of old, cf. Ezra 7:6, 11), these issues in Paul's writings remain unclear to the average reader.

Third, *the perspicuity of Scripture does not mean all Scripture is equally clear to any one individual.* Even well-read scholars are known to say such things as, 'I'm not clear as to what this passage means', or, 'There are several possible interpretations of this passage of Scripture, all of which fulfill the criteria of sound exegesis and principles of interpretation.'

Fourth, *the perspicuity of Scripture means that all the 'essential' truths necessary for salvation are clearly propounded somewhere in Scripture.* Not all truth that the Bible teaches is necessary for the purposes of salvation. There are truths which are, as Paul suggests, 'first of all':

> For I delivered to you *as of first importance* what I also received: that Christ died for our sins in accordance with the Scriptures, that he was buried, that he was raised on the third day in accordance with the Scriptures (1 Cor. 15:3, 4).

The truths of Christ's substitutionary death, burial, and resurrection are considered as *primary* truths. The Bible also teaches a vast array of truths – such as the millennium (Rev. 20), women's head-covering (1 Cor. 11), the identity of Behemoth and Leviathan (Job 40–41) – which are not vital to know or understand in order to be saved. This 'hierarchy of truths' (as it is sometimes called) is an important concept in itself. There are matters which are *primary*, and there are matters which are *secondary* and *tertiary*.

Fifth, *the perspicuity of Scripture does not mean that readers don't require help from others (more expert) in order to make sense of it.*

Two issues arise here that we need to consider: first of all, the role of 'teachers' in our understanding of Scripture – what the *Westminster Confession* included in the phrase 'the ordinary means' in the citation above. The reformers of the sixteenth-century Reformation spoke strongly against the tyranny of a medieval church that seemed to deliberately withhold Scripture from the ordinary people. But the the reformers' protest was not a denial that God gives the gift of insight to certain people who will then help others come to a better understanding of his word. Paul reminded the Ephesians that the risen Lord 'gave the apostles, the prophets, the evangelists, the pastors and teachers, to equip the saints for the work of ministry' (Eph. 4:11-12). This statement reflects an understanding of the role of gifted individuals in helping all the saints come to an understanding of the truth and the tasks assigned to them (verses 13-16). Preachers, Bible study leaders, Sunday School teachers, and so on, help us understand the Bible. This places an extraordinary burden on those who teach Scripture in whatever form that may take. Teachers need to avoid the tendency that manifests itself in the overuse of technical terms (without explanation) or the citation of Greek and Hebrew in a manner that suggests that ordinary folk are not to be trusted with a Bible in their own hands. There is a subtlety in teaching (and preaching too!) that can all too easily revert to the obscuring of vital spiritual truths that was associated with the medieval church. The perspicuity of Scripture should constrain teachers of the Bible to be clear and succinct in the essential matters. Indeed, one of the measures of a successful Bible study or sermon is the idea (whether true or not) that one could have seen the lesson of the study or sermon without the aid of a teacher! In reality, the hearer probably could not have done so without a teacher, but such was the clarity of the instruction that it felt as though the teacher was largely redundant. Pride (on the part of teachers) makes this a very difficult pill to swallow.

Knowing intellectually and knowing savingly

The second issue that arises from what we have just considered is our need to distinguish between an 'understanding' and a '*saving* understanding' of the Scriptures. The Ethiopian in Acts 8 could read the scroll of Isaiah which he had purchased in Jerusalem, and presumably could understand some of it. But the true significance of what he read was lost on him. There is the vital role Philip played in asking the astute question, 'Do you understand what you are reading?' (Acts 8:30). And there is the equally honest answer of the Ethiopian, 'How can I, unless someone guides me?' (verse 31). Philip then got into the chariot and began to interpret Isaiah 53 – the passage the Ethiopian had difficulty understanding. Philip 'told him the good news about Jesus' (verse 35). And the Ethiopian received it by faith and was saved. Clearly, there is the role of Philip as evangelist and teacher. But there is also the role of the Holy Spirit as illuminator of the text of Scripture and the One who enabled the Ethiopian to see the key interpretive issue of the Scripture under consideration – *Jesus*!

What, then, have we learned about the perspicuity of Scripture?

- All we need to know in order to love God and serve him faithfully is found in Scripture.
- All that is essential for us to know is clearly given somewhere in Scripture.
- The Lord employs other people to help us understand the Scripture.
- We require the illumination of the Holy Spirit to properly come to a saving understanding of Scripture.

11

The Interpretation of Scripture

Do your best to come to me soon. – 2 Timothy 4:9

Words have meaning. To understand the meaning of words – words by themselves as well as in relation to other words – requires the employment of a set of strict principles and rules of interpretation. Without these, the interpretation of Scripture is subject to all manner of flights of fancy through the spiritualizing, moralizing, or allegorizing of the text and its meaning.

Paul told Timothy, 'Do your best to present yourself to God as one approved, a worker who has no need to be ashamed, rightly handling the word of truth' (2 Tim. 2:15). The verb 'do your best' (cf. 2 Tim. 4:9) suggests effort and hard work. It is a word that was also used to describe the laborious task of road construction. In other words, rightly handling and interpreting the Bible is hard work! It is so very easy to get it wrong.

The first rule of interpretation is that Scripture must be interpreted *literally*. The meaning of words and sentences is to be understood within the context in which they were written. We need to ask, What did this word mean at the time it was employed? Adhering to a 'grammatical-historical' method of interpretation will help us avoid falling into the danger of engaging in fanciful allegorizing the text of Scripture. This rule fully recognizes that within the Scriptures there is a variety of different literary genres: history, law, proverb, parable, poetry, apocalyptic, gospel, apostolic correspondence, and even allegory. Identifying the precise kind of literature and the distinct rules that apply to each is vital to sound interpretation. Apocalyptic literature – the second half of Daniel and most of the book of Revelation, for example, employs the use of distinctive tools to convey meaning – vivid colours, numbers, exaggerated and startling images, and such like. Knowing the kind of literature under consideration will enable us to focus on what is central, rather than on what is merely intended as 'filler' in conveying the larger, graphic point.

Often the term 'literal' is used in a negative and contemptuous way by those who sneer at conservative evangelicals who believe the Bible should be interpreted as teaching such things as a literal Adam and Eve, a parting of the Red Sea, or the raising of Lazarus who had been dead for four days. But the term is still useful. One way to respond to the question, 'Do you believe the Bible to be literally true?' is to answer, 'Yes! I understand the Bible according to the rules of the literature it contains. I interpret history as history, parable as parable, apocalyptic as apocalyptic, etc., interpreting each genre differently.'

The second rule of interpretation is that *Scripture must interpret itself*, what is often referred to as the *analogy of Scripture*. The logic is flawless. If the Bible is the infallible word of God, no greater authority can be introduced to provide its ultimate meaning – not that of church councils, popes, or the 'reason' or 'intuition' of fallible men and women. It is for this reason that Bibles often include (as aids to interpretation) cross-references to other verses or passages in Scripture which cast light on the text. Certain parts of the Bible seem to bring together vast amounts of Scripture and in effect provide us with God's own interpretation on entire threads of meaning. Paul's letter to the Romans is one such example. In a dedication prefaced to his commentary on this letter, Calvin wrote: 'if we understand this Epistle, we have a passage opened to us to the understanding of the whole of scripture'.[1]

A third rule of interpretation is the rule of *non-contradiction*. Scripture cannot contradict itself. It is a corollary to the Bible's inerrancy. The Bible is God's word. When the Bible speaks, God speaks. God cannot contradict himself; therefore the Bible cannot contradict itself. There are times, of course, when the Bible *appears* to be doing just that. When Moses announced a law allowing divorce (Deut. 24:1), it appears to contradict an earlier law of creation that marriage was only dissolved by death – 'till death us do part' (cf. Gen. 2:24). For this very reason, Jesus himself

[1] John Calvin, *Epistles of Paul the Apostle to the Romans and to the Thessalonians*, vol. 38: *Romans*, tr. Ros MacKenzie (Edinburgh: Oliver and Boyd, 1960), p. 2.

provides an explanation, that Moses added a toleration of divorce (through the Holy Spirit's inspiration) 'because of your hardness of heart' (Matt. 19:8).

No one part of Scripture can be set against another part of Scripture. The principle commits us, in advance, to a principle of harmonization. We will consider this issue again, when we ask questions about difficulties in interpreting certain parts of Scripture. The point here is to insist on a method of approach which avoids any conclusion that the Bible is mistaken when dealing with difficulties in the text.

A fourth rule of interpretation is to understand that, in the words of the Westminster Confession of Faith, the meaning of Scripture is '*not manifold, but one*'. In the context of the *Confession* and the theological debates of the sixteenth century, this statement was meant to address the so-called 'medieval quadriga', or fourfold rule of interpretation, by which Scripture was subjected to four different meanings (at the same time). In addition to the *literal* sense, Scripture also had to have a *moral*, *allegorical*, and *analogical* sense. Jerusalem, for example, could refer to the city and capital of Judea, the soul of man, the church, and also heaven. Such was the enthusiasm for the allegorical and analogical[1] interpretations that the literal meaning was often trivialized or ignored altogether.

The phrase 'not manifold, but one' has a peculiar relevance to our own, late-modern era. As we saw earlier in

[1] The analogical meaning was closely related to the allegorical meaning but drew upon an interpretation that considered the heavenly (eschatological) pilgrimage.

chapter 2, as a consequence of the denial of objective truth, a word now means, as Lewis Carroll's Humpty Dumpty so famously expressed it, 'just what I choose it to mean – neither more nor less'.[1] The question 'Is there meaning in the text?' has become something of an uncertain quest which too often reaches a conclusion based on nothing more than personal preference influenced by prejudice, sentiment, and feeling. The rule which insists that the meaning of Scripture is '*not manifold, but one*' is a remonstration against such subjective interpretations. The study of the Bible ought never to rely on an interpretive guideline which is ordered by the sentiment, '*I like to think that what this text means is …*'

Three keys

In addition to the rules of interpretation outlined above, several essential keys are needed to rightly handle the word of God.[2]

The first is *context*. Scripture is written in sentences with a logical flow and sequence of thought.

To demonstrate the importance of context, let us take the use of the word 'flesh' (Greek, *sarx*) as an example. In Paul's writings the term is synonymous with the idea of man's fallen condition and sin. 'For the desires of the *flesh* are against the Spirit', Paul tells the Galatians (Gal. 5:17). But in John's writings the word has a very different meaning.

[1] See page 14 above, footnote 1.

[2] For a fuller expansion on these keys, see Sinclair B. Ferguson, *From the Mouth of God*, pp. 71-82.

When this apostle tells us in his prologue that 'the Word became *flesh* and dwelt among us' (John 1:14), he does not intend to say that Jesus became a fallen human being, united to Adam in the consequences of his sin. Jesus was without sin, *sinless* (cf. John 7:18; Heb. 4:15). Knowing the context of the word *flesh* is therefore vital to interpret its meaning correctly.

The second key is *Jesus*. From Genesis 3:15 onwards, it is clear that the thread of the narrative that holds Scripture together is the provision of a Saviour who will redeem the people of God from the debt and bondage of sin. Jesus made it clear that the central theme of the Old Testament was *himself*. Speaking to a Jewish audience, he said, 'You search the Scriptures because you think that in them you have eternal life; and it is *they that bear witness about me*' (John 5:39). Similarly, with two dejected disciples making their way home to Emmaus from Jerusalem, Jesus took them through a Bible study which covered every part of the Hebrew Bible: 'beginning with Moses and all the Prophets, he interpreted to them in all the Scriptures the things concerning himself' (Luke 24:27). This is not to suggest that the *only* meaning of any particular text of Scripture is Jesus. The text, for example, may be an exhortation that requires a specific response. But underlying the exhortation is the knowledge that the only way that response is possible is due to the fact that by God's grace a saving relation with Jesus has been established in the life of the believer.

Jesus is the key to everything in Scripture. He is its central message.

The third key is the *divine plot line*. This is particularly important when interpreting historical portions of the Old Testament. Whether we are in the graphic and bloody period of the Judges, or the sublime narrative of Ruth, or in Babylon with the exiles, we must keep in mind the reason for this history, which is ultimately to tell the tale of how Jesus was to be born in Bethlehem.

Often, the promise of God to Abraham – that Abraham would be the father of many nations and that his descendants would be more numerous than the stars in the night sky (Gen. 15:5) – appears to have failed. But again and again, the promise holds true. We must always keep the 'big picture' in view when interpreting Scripture. We must ask, 'How does this part of the unfolding story fulfil the promise of redemption in the coming of Jesus Christ?'

Of course, there is another perspective too. And the history must not lose sight of the fact that God uses people's twisted, sinful, failing lives to accomplish his purpose – lives that often uncannily reflect our own, and from which we may learn many valuable lessons about discipleship in the face of dark providences in a sinful world. Both perspectives are necessary if we are to rightly handle the word of God.

We will address this issue in greater detail in the next chapter.

12

The Central Message of Scripture

... that the Son of Man must be delivered into the hands of sinful men and be crucified and on the third day rise.

—Luke 24:7

In the previous chapter, we suggested that one key which unlocks the meaning of the Bible is *Jesus*. According to Jesus the Old Testament Scriptures 'bear witness' to him (John 5:39). Eternal life does not come from merely possessing the Scriptures but from possessing the Christ to whom the Scriptures bear witness. The importance of this is seen in the way the risen Lord ministered the word to the two forlorn disciples on the road to Emmaus. 'And beginning with Moses and all the Prophets, he interpreted to them in all the Scriptures the things concerning himself' (Luke 24:27). Faith 'comes from hearing, and hearing through the *word of Christ*' (Rom. 10:17).

Of course, the Bible is more than a book about Jesus. Summarizing, we could say that the Bible serves a fourfold purpose:

First, the Bible provides us with a description of the triune God – the 'three-personed God', the Father, the Son and the Holy Spirit – the Creator, Sustainer, Redeemer, and Judge. In this sense the Bible is God-centred. Scripture records the things which God would have us know about *himself* – his character, attributes, works, decisions, plans, promises, and much more. As we saw in chapter 1, God has revealed himself in creation, redemption, and judgment:

> For what can be known about God is plain to them, because God has shown it to them. For his invisible attributes, namely, his eternal power and divine nature, have been clearly perceived, ever since the creation of the world, in the things that have been made (Rom. 1:19, 20).

And God has also spoken and revealed his saving and redemptive purposes to us through his prophets and ultimately and most especially 'by his Son':

> Long ago, at many times and in many ways, God spoke to our fathers by the prophets, but in these last days he has spoken to us by his Son, whom he appointed the heir of all things, through whom also he created the world. He is the radiance of the glory of God and the exact imprint of his nature, and he upholds the universe by the word of his power (Heb. 1:1-3).

Yet it is vital for us to remember that, though we are the recipients of this wonderful revelation, our knowledge of God and his ways is not complete or full. We know in part for God has revealed *only a little*. He is too great for us to understand. God has spoken to us in what might be called 'baby-talk'.[1] In other words, he has accommodated himself to the smallness of finite minds.

Second, the Bible is a training manual for redeemed sinners. It directs them to 'renounce ungodliness and worldly passions, and to live self-controlled, upright, and godly lives in the present age' (Titus 2:11, 12). The Bible guides us in our evangelism, worship, and service. It instructs us on the way of salvation, insisting that salvation is 'apart from works' (Rom. 3:28). It shows us what godliness looks like, insisting on the absolute necessity of 'the obedience of faith' (Rom. 1:5; 16:26), and that without works all professions of faith are empty and dead (James 2:26).

Third, the Bible traces the flow of the history of redemption, showing how God's plan of salvation reveals itself in the intricate nuances of the narratives of the Old and New Testaments. It speaks of a divine covenant of grace, forged in eternity and manifested at various significant staging posts in human history (Abraham, Moses, David, and in the prophets, a promise of a *new* covenant). Knowing where we are in this historical plot line is important to finding our way to the *main* message of Scripture.

Fourth, and fundamentally, the Bible is about the provision of God's Son as Saviour and Redeemer for lost and perishing sinners. Jesus, promised in the types, shadows, and prophecies of the Old Testament; Jesus, the God-man, crucified, risen, ascended, and coming again in glory – is the Bible's central focus throughout.

[1] Cf. John Calvin, *Institutes*, I.iii.14.

From a human point of view, the Bible has *many* authors. From a divine point of view, the Bible has *one* author – God the Holy Spirit. It stands to reason, therefore, that the message of Scripture is a unified message. God has a divine will and purpose. He has set it forth in Christ: 'a plan for the fullness of time, to unite all things in him, things in heaven and things on earth' (Eph. 1:9, 10). This divine plan has its roots in the beginning:

> … remember the former things of old;
> for I am God, and there is no other;
> I am God, and there is none like me,
> declaring the end from the beginning
> and from ancient times things not yet done,
> saying, 'My counsel shall stand,
> and I will accomplish all my purpose' (Isa. 46:9, 10).

And Paul gathers this promise together and says:

> When the fullness of time had come, God sent forth his Son, born of woman, born under the law, to redeem those who were under the law, so that we might receive adoption as sons (Gal. 4:4, 5).

The coming of Jesus – his taking human flesh, life of obedience, crucifixion, burial, resurrection, and ascension – form the mid-point of history. Despite political correctness, there is a reason why history has been viewed as BC (*before* Christ) and AD (*after* Christ).[1] The entire Bible can

[1] The term *anno Domini* is Medieval Latin and means 'in the year of the Lord', and is taken from the full original phrase '*anno Domini nostri Jesu Christi*', which translates to 'in the year of our Lord Jesus Christ'. 'The

be viewed from this perspective: promises *made*, promises *kept*.[1] Summing up vast amounts of Old Testament Scripture, Paul writes to the Corinthians, 'For all the promises of God find their Yes in him' (2 Cor. 1:20). In summary:

> Because the dominant plot line of the whole Bible is what God accomplishes through his Son, and in the power of the Holy Spirit, from start to finish these sixty-six books tell *a single, multifaceted story whose central character is Jesus Christ and what he does*. He is the one through whom all things were created, in whom all things hold together, and by whom God brings reconciliation.[2]

The Bible, therefore, tells a coherent story. True, there are repetitions, parallel narratives, and the occasional borrowing from one book to another, but the narrative remains unified. God is at the centre throughout; his people, his covenant, his kingdom (God as king ruling over his people), and what is more, God's King – his Son, Jesus Christ, to whom he has given all authority in heaven and earth. The Bible also records this narrative in terms of the effect of the Redeemer's work: he redeems, forgives, and

work of Christ on earth, and especially his crucifixion and resurrection, is the climax of history; it is the great turning point at which God actually accomplished the salvation toward which history had been moving throughout the Old Testament.' Vern S. Poythress, 'A Survey of the History of Salvation', in *Understanding Scripture*, p. 170.

[1] Note the titles of two books by Mark Dever, *The Message of the Old Testament: Promises Made* (Wheaton, IL: Crossway, 2006), *The Message of the New Testament: Promises Kept* (Wheaton, IL: Crossway, 2005).

[2] Sinclair B. Ferguson, *From the Mouth of God*, p. 76. Cf. John 1:1-3; Col. 1:16, 17, 20.

calls sinners to a life of godliness (which includes faith, repentance, obedience, mortification of sin, prayer, worship of God, joy, love, and assured hope), by the power of the Holy Spirit, so that they will reflect the King's image (cf. Rom. 8:29).

To read the Bible and to grasp its central truth and message requires something which all readers of the Bible must ask the Holy Spirit to provide. Martin Luther was correct when he said that the one thing Bible readers must do to understand Scripture is to pray for the illumination of the Holy Spirit.[1] And when the Spirit comes in his illuminating power he will show us the central message of Scripture by shining 'in our hearts to give us the light of the knowledge of *the glory of God in the face of Jesus Christ*' (2 Cor. 4:6).

[1] 'Nobody who has not the Spirit of God sees a jot of what is in the Scriptures. ... The Spirit is needed for the understanding of all Scripture and every part of Scripture.' Martin Luther, *The Bondage of the Will*, pp. 73, 74.

13

The Application of Scripture

All Scripture is breathed out by God and profitable for teaching, for reproof, for correction, and for training in righteousness, that the man of God may be competent, equipped for every good work. – 2 Timothy 3:16, 17

Rightly understanding and interpreting Scripture should have a profound effect upon us.

First, it will affect our thinking and knowing. Scripture is profitable '*for teaching*'. It is a mistake to think that 'application' of Scripture consists solely in verbs involving 'doing' and 'responding' in what we customarily refer to as some 'practical' way. Before any of that takes place, we need to know certain things. Part of the application of Scripture, indeed, its primary function, is to change the way we think. We need a change of *mind* – we need to change the way we *think* about God, about ourselves, and about the world in which we live. Scripture is God's sword (Eph. 6:17). With it we are meant to slay ideas that promote incorrect behaviour. It is vital to grasp this lest we fall into the error of thinking that application only comes at the end of a Bible study or sermon. Grasping the truth and being caught up in it, with awe and joy, is itself application. Paul reminds Timothy that 'God may perhaps grant them [those who oppose the gospel] repentance leading to a knowledge of the truth' (2 Tim. 2:25), though some will be 'always learning' but 'never able to arrive at a knowledge of the truth' (2 Tim. 3:7). Our minds matter. What we *think* is vital to holiness.

But equally, the Scriptures are profitable for '*reproof*'; Scripture rebukes and convicts. It troubles our conscience. It shows us our sins. It exposes our ungodliness.

Scripture also '*corrects*'. The word Paul uses here – *epanorthōsis* – refers to the retracting of a statement in order to correct it or intensify it. An example would be, 'Thousands, no, *millions* of people live in London!' The root of the word ('*ortho-*') refers to the idea of straightening. That part of the word has been brought into English from the Greek (think of an orthodontist – someone who straightens teeth). Scripture 'straightens' us and (as with orthodontists) makes us appear more beautiful.

Scripture is also useful for '*training in righteousness*'. Godliness requires training, or discipline. Though not the verb employed here, the Greek does employ another word, *gumnazō*, also translated 'train', from which we easily recognize the English word *gymnasium.*[1] Scripture sends us to the gym.

[1] Cf. Heb. 5:14.

The point is this: the purpose of the Bible is to change the way we think and behave. When reading and studying the Bible we should ask ourselves a number of questions which will assist this process of change:

- What does this passage teach me about truth?
- What is this passage asking me to believe?
- What is this passage teaching me about God?
- What does this passage teach me about the gospel?
- What does it teach me about myself?
- What does this passage teach me about relating to other people?
- What does this passage say about my responsibilities?
- How does this passage relate to my desires and ambitions?

And perhaps, most basically:

- What does this passage tell me *to do*?

Avoiding Pharisaism

A warning is necessary when considering the application of Scripture. We are Pharisees by nature, hard-wired to self-justification. Our doing can so easily revert to a 'works-based' mentality of trying to earn God's favour *in order to be* in a right relationship with him. This was the mindset of the older brother who fell into a sulk because of the way the father welcomed home his wayward son: 'Look, these many years I have served you, and I never disobeyed your command, yet you never gave me a young goat, that I might celebrate with my friends' (Luke 15:29). The word 'served' can, and in all likelihood should, be rendered 'slaved'. The obedience offered by the older son (and note he was already a 'son') was viewed as 'slavery'. He had failed to grasp his status as a son.

It is all too possible that obedience (the *application* demanded by Scripture) will be viewed as a form of slavery, demands made in order to be justified (or, perhaps, to be *further* justified). But this is to misunderstand justification. Faith in Christ, 'apart from the works of the law', renders us law-keepers and covenant-keepers. As a result, we are considered adopted sons and heirs – heirs together with Christ (Gal. 4:1-7; Rom. 8:14-17). There is nothing that we can *do* that will further enable our justification.

Faith also renders us *positionally* (*legally* or *definitively*) sanctified, or holy. Paul addresses the Corinthians as 'the church of God that is in Corinth, to those *sanctified* in Christ Jesus, called to be *saints*' (1 Cor. 1:2). In Christ, we are saints! We are regarded as holy. Any obedience we offer, therefore, is in response to this truth about ourselves. It is gratitude in action. The imperative (the 'do this' or 'don't do that' of Scripture) is based on the indicative – what we *already are in union with Christ*. None of this lessens the force of the imperatives. There remains a divine necessity for holiness to be worked out in our lives: 'without [holiness] no one will see the Lord' (Heb. 12:14).

The shape of holiness is twofold: *negatively*, there are sins – sins of thought and action, shaped by recurring patterns (habits) of behavioural response to stimuli – that need to be 'put to death' (Rom. 8:13; Col. 3:5). *Positively*, there is the ninefold fruit of the Spirit ('love, joy, peace, patience, kindness, goodness, faithfulness, gentleness, self-control', Gal. 5:22-24), which needs to be cultivated and nurtured into visible and sustainable life.

Such holiness requires effort and hard work on our part – faith-fuelled, Spirit-enabled, and gospel-driven effort, but effort nevertheless. And the danger of falling back into sin and, yes, into apostasy is all too possible. Hence the apostle Paul's use of such energy-demanding words as 'toil', 'strive', and 'fight'. And was it not the Lord Jesus himself who told his hearers to '*strive* to enter through the narrow door' (Luke 13:24; 1 Tim. 4:10; 6:12)?

The petitions of the Lord's Prayer – the model prayer Jesus taught his disciples to follow – remind us that in our constant battle against the evil one, we have daily need of forgiveness and divine protection. The mystery of the Christian life is that Christ expects us to flee from sin and the devil, but does not expect us to rid ourselves of either on this side of glory. Repentance is the way of life, as is the pursuit of godliness. As Martin Luther taught the world in the first of his Ninety-Five Theses nailed to the door of the Castle Church, Wittenberg, on October 31, 1517: 'When our Lord and Master Jesus Christ said "Repent", he intended that the *entire life* of believers should be repentance.'

This gospel-driven *effort* on our part, in response to the teaching of Scripture, is nothing but an expression of our desire to become more like our Saviour with whom we are already united. Here, in this world, we walk between two worlds: the *now* and the *not yet* – 'we are God's children now, and what we will be has not yet appeared; but we know that when he appears we shall be like him, because we shall see him as he is' (1 John 3:2). With Paul, we find ourselves exasperated by our actions: 'For I do not understand my own actions. For I do not do what I want, but I do the very thing I hate' (Rom. 7:15). Daily, therefore, we strive to apply the Bible to our whole beings – mind, will, affection, and disposition – saying in response to all that we read: 'What shall *I do*, Lord?' (Acts 22:10).

Hearers and doers

Knowing what the Bible says is never enough. This was a point driven home by the Lord when he told his disciples in the Upper Room: 'If you know these things, blessed are you if you do them' (John 13:17). The blessing is attached, not to the *knowing*, but to the *doing* of the things he has taught and commanded.

It is in the letter of James that we see the Lord's teaching on this matter most clearly applied: 'Be doers of the word, and not hearers only' (James 1:22). Bible study that doesn't result in changed *thought* and *action* is an exercise in futility. Scripture equips us 'for every good work' (2 Tim. 3:17).

The puritan minister and author Thomas Watson (*c.* 1620–86) gave advice which is as pertinent today as it was when first given more than four centuries ago:

> Take every word as spoken to yourselves. When the word thunders against sin, think thus: 'God means my sins'; when it presseth any duty, 'God intends me in this.' Many put off Scripture from themselves, as if it only concerned

> those who lived in the time when it was written; but if you intend to profit by the word, bring it home to yourselves: a medicine will do no good, unless it be applied.[1]

When the Lord commissioned Joshua to be leader of the people of Israel following the death of Moses, he spoke to him about the crucial importance of reading and applying Scripture in these well-known words:

> This Book of the Law shall not depart from your mouth, but you shall meditate on it day and night, so that you may be careful to do according to all that is written in it. For then you will make your way prosperous, and then you will have good success (Josh. 1:8).

In these words the Lord highlights three distinct features:

- First, Scripture affects our minds and hearts.
- Second, it motivates behaviour and action.
- Third, it brings blessing upon careful obedience.

Applying God's words to our lives is an experience of grace and a means of experiencing ongoing grace.

'If you know these things, blessed are you
if you do them' (John 13:17).

[1] Cited by Donald S. Whitney, *Spiritual Disciplines for the Christian Life* (Colorado Springs: NavPress, 2014), p. 57.

Further Reading

Where to start

Sinclair B. Ferguson, *From the Mouth of God: Trusting, Reading, and Applying the Bible* (Banner of Truth Trust, 2014)

J. I. Packer, *Fundamentalism and the Word of God* (Eerdmans, 1972)

E. J. Young, *Thy Word Is Truth* (Banner of Truth Trust, 2012)

R. C. Sproul, *Knowing Scripture* (IVP, 2009)

In more detail

John MacArthur (ed.), *The Inerrant Word: Biblical, Historical, Theological, and Pastoral Perspectives* (Crossway, 2016)

Wayne Grudem, C. John Collins, and Thomas Schreiner (eds.), *Understanding Scripture: An Overview of the Bible's Origin, Reliability, and Meaning* (Crossway, 2012)

Michael J. Kruger, *Canon Revisited: Establishing the Origins and Authority of the New Testament Books* (Crossway, 2012); and *The Question of Canon: Challenging the Status Quo in the New Testament Debate* (IVP Academic, 2013)

Philip Wesley Comfort (ed.), *The Origin of the Bible* (Tyndale House Publishers, 2003)

David J. Murray, *Jesus on Every Page: 10 Simple Ways to Seek and Find Christ in the Old Testament* (Thomas Nelson Publishers, 2013)

The bigger picture

Peter A. Lillback & Richard B. Gaffin Jr. (eds.), *Thy Word Is Still Truth: Essential Writings on the Doctrine of Scripture from the Reformation to Today* (P & R Publishing, 2013)

G. K. Beale, *The Erosion of Inerrancy in Evangelicalism: Responding to Challenges to Biblical Authority* (Crossway, 2008)

Banner Mini-Guides

The Bible: God's Inerrant Word
Derek W. H. Thomas

The Christian Mind: Escaping Futility
William Edgar

The Church: Glorious Body, Radiant Bride
Mark G. Johnston

Growing in Grace: Becoming More Like Jesus
Jonathan Master

Regeneration: Made New by the Spirit of God
David B. McWilliams

Salvation: Full and Free in Christ
Ian Hamilton

Sanctification: Transformed Life
David Campbell